P9-CRL-662

The Girl in

the Photograph

Also by Byron L. Dorgan

*Take This Job and Ship It: How Corporate Greed and
Brain-Dead Politics Are Selling Out America*

*Reckless!: How Debt, Deregulation, and Dark Money Nearly
Bankrupted America (And How We Can Fix It!)*

Gridlock (with David Hagberg)

Blowout (with David Hagberg)

The Girl in the Photograph

Byron L. Dorgan

Thomas Dunne Books
New York

First published in the United States by Thomas Dunne Books,
an imprint of St. Martin's Publishing Group

THE GIRL IN THE PHOTOGRAPH. Copyright © 2019 by
Byron L. Dorgan. All rights reserved. Printed in the United States of
America. For information, address St. Martin's Publishing Group,
120 Broadway, New York, NY 10271.

www.thomasdunnebooks.com

Designed by Devan Norman

Frontispiece photo by Tom Stromme, Bismarck Tribune Co.

The Library of Congress Cataloging-in-Publication
Data is available upon request.

ISBN 978-1-250-17364-5 (hardcover)
ISBN 978-1-250-17365-2 (ebook)

Our books may be purchased in bulk for promotional,
educational, or business use. Please contact your local bookseller
or the Macmillan Corporate and Premium Sales Department
at 1-800-221-7945, extension 5442, or by email at
MacmillanSpecialMarkets@macmillan.com.

First Edition: November 2019

10 9 8 7 6 5 4 3 2 1

Contents

Acknowledgments   *ix*

Introduction   *1*

1. The Lost Girl   *9*

2. A People Under Siege   *19*

3. The Kindness of a Stranger   *32*

4. There's Little Care in This Health Care System   *55*

5. Teach the Children Well   *81*

6. Justice Is a Stranger Here   *100*

7. The Next Generation of Leaders   *117*

8. Leadership   *135*

9. Defenders of the Earth   *155*

10. The Arc of the Moral Universe Is Bending Toward Justice   *168*

11. New Opportunities   *178*

What You Can Do   *195*

Acknowledgments

This book could not have been written without the coopera-tion of a young woman named Tamara, who, in her first email to me, said that if telling her story could be helpful to other Native American youth, she appreciated that I had told the difficult story of her early life. For this book, Tamara coop-erated in telling me her story in terms that I am sure were often painful for her. But she wanted her story to be told in ways that could help other Native American children.

I know her experiences, as tragic as they have been, are not unique. There are other young Native American youth who are now experiencing the same trauma, difficulty, and challenges. The candor offered by Tamara in telling her story is a gift to others going through those same difficulties. It is a message about survival and overcoming obstacles.

I know Tamara to be a wonderful person, full of compassion and continuing to search for opportunities to improve her life.

Tamara's struggles have not been of her own making. The

burdens she now carries were visited upon her at a very young age. As this book was written, she found more stability in her life, and I am hopeful that she will have good health, happiness, and a brighter future. I dedicate this book to a remarkable young woman with a spirit I deeply admire. Her name is Tamara, and she is the girl in the photograph!

I also want to acknowledge the special collaboration I have had with Tony Bender, a brilliant editor and writer whose work I have long admired. His contributions to create this book and help tell Tamara's story have been invaluable.

Finally, to my wife, Kim, who has been so wonderfully patient as I worked to complete this book. Thank you for understanding my passion about this story. You have been my constant inspiration for more than thirty years.

The Girl in

the Photograph

Introduction

Humankind has not woven the web of life.
We are but one thread within it.
Whatever we do to the web, we do to ourselves.
All things are bound together.
All things connect.

—CHIEF SEATTLE

Often we don't choose our journey; the journey chooses us. That's how this book began.

In 1990, I was reading *The Bismarck Tribune* at my desk in my U.S. congressional office in Washington, D.C. The front page included a story headlined: FOSTER HOME CHILDREN BEATEN— AND NOBODY'S HELPING. It was about a girl named Tamara from the Standing Rock Indian Reservation who had been so horrifically beaten in a foster home when she was two, that, three years later, she was in full emotional retreat. According to her grandfather, she spent her time huddling in the shadows, singing television jingles as if they were hymns that might bring her into the light.

The article posed the question, "Are Indian children being seized from their parents by Bureau of Indian Affairs social workers and practically sold into servitude as a way for the social workers' acquaintances to collect a foster care paycheck?" With rampant unemployment on the Indian reservation, had children become a government-sanctioned commodity?

The story was captivating. The questions were very important to me as a member of Congress from North Dakota, which has a large Native American population. But what captivated me was the large color picture that accompanied the story.

There she was, Tamara, a beautiful five-year-old with a short bowl haircut, hands clasped as if in prayer, glancing warily at the camera, a single tear running down her cheek, caught in limbo, certainly in darkness, facing an uncertain future. And so it is with too many children on the reservation.

That tear. It's not possible to see that photograph without it being seared into your consciousness. Oh, life can change you in an instant, all right. Tamara's life had been forever altered. So had mine.

According to the story, "a Bureau of Indian Affairs Social Services document shows that Tamara's mother had her five children taken from her by court order after accusations of child neglect." At Tamara's foster home, safety was an illusion. She could have died.

During what was described as a drunken party at that home, she suffered massive injuries. Her leg, arm, and nose were broken, and some of her hair was pulled out at the roots. She lay suffering alone in a dark room for several days before social services officials arrived at the home and demanded to see her.

The *Tribune* story described how the social services representative finally rescued Tamara: "As a foster child, Tamara was enrolled in the Fort Yates infant development program. Everything was fine at first. But then the case manager was denied access to the foster home for two weeks. Finally, she went to the foster home with two other social workers. They heard a radio, but nobody answered the door. After repeated knocking, they were finally let into the house.

"At first the foster family wouldn't let the social workers into the bedroom where Tamara was laying. They said she had chicken pox. 'They let us see Tamara after about fifteen minutes,' the case manager said. 'She was bruised all over. Her leg was wrapped in an Ace bandage. Something was wrong with her arm . . . her toes were swollen.'

"'I told them we would have to take her to the Fort Yates hospital . . . It seemed like she'd shut down. You'd look into her eyes and it was like she wasn't there.'"

Her grandfather was a former tribal policeman who, according to the newspaper story, was attempting to take legal action against the Bureau of Indian Affairs for what had been done to his grandchildren.

The news story reported when the children were removed from their home because of child neglect, they were placed in a foster home in the household of an extended family member.

According to the story, the two older children ran away from the foster home. One of them was caught and locked in a basement room with a Doberman pinscher.

Tamara's grandfather, who was still reeling over the loss of another five grandchildren in a fire, said, "There was a crime that occurred here. Human beings were abused. But nothing was done."

Just another day in a forgotten corner of America?

It was impossible for me to read the story, look at the photo, and then set it aside. The photo of Tamara gnawed at me. It held great power.

Even before I read that story, I had long known of the danger that some foster homes on Indian reservations held for some children. Yes, I know many were loving homes that served the needs of the children in a safe and competent manner, but there were also others that failed. Horribly.

I had worked over many years in Congress to help Indian tribes find the resources to address serious problems, including the issue of safeguarding Indian children who were placed in foster care. It hadn't been enough. It certainly wasn't enough to offer safety to a two-year-old child whose serious injuries would plague her for the rest of her life.

Enraged, I suppose, would be the best description of my emotions as I read the story over and over again, riveted for minutes at a time by the sad photograph. I was determined to find out how this could have happened and how we could stop it from happening in the future.

A child was severely beaten, and no one was charged for committing the crime. Someone had to answer for this.

The very next weekend after reading the newspaper story, I traveled to the Standing Rock Indian Reservation to meet with Tamara and her grandfather. She was sitting on his lap staring at the floor. She didn't speak and didn't even seem to notice I was in the room.

Then I met with tribal officials and social services workers on the reservation. I learned that the child welfare system on the reservation had caseworkers assigned to an absurd number of child welfare cases. They were ridiculously understaffed and could not possibly assure the safety of all the kids they were responsible for placing in foster homes.

So I launched an inquiry. I demanded answers. But there were no good ones, just lame excuses and finger-pointing all around.

Following my visit to the Indian reservation, I kept in touch with Tamara and sent her notes along with Christmas gifts over the next couple of years. But when her grandfather died, I lost track of her. I inquired about her from time to time when I would travel to the Indian reservation for my work as a congressman and then a senator from North Dakota, but no one seemed to know what had become of the young girl. She just seemed to disappear.

I kept the *Tribune* story and the photograph of Tamara in my desk drawer for nearly three decades. I would come across it from time to time while going through the desk drawer, and I wondered what became of that little girl whose life had begun with such tragedy.

Then, twenty-seven years later, I got a message from the most surprising direction and learned the rest of the amazing story.

Tamara's journey is about how she's dealt with adversity. It is also a clear-eyed account of the circumstances, issues, and conditions she and too many other Native American youth face every day, a microcosm of the inequities and shortcomings of this great country that extend far beyond Indian reservations. Hers—and theirs—is not an easy story, but it is not without hope.

It's important to understand that tribal governments, parents, teachers, and many others important in the lives of young Native Americans have made and continue to make valiant efforts to effect positive change. This book only includes a fraction of those stories. But it is an undeniable fact that despite those efforts, too many First Americans have been left behind. And that's especially true of Native American youth, many of whom have been caught up in a cycle of despair. A dull ache permeates the souls of many of these young Americans. And the tragedy of teen suicide on Indian reservations is one manifestation of those conditions.

One tragedy of our times is the unending headlines in our country about school shootings. Yet in this book, you will hear from a teacher who lost thirteen of her Native American students to suicide in eight years. There were no headlines about that.

This book tells the story of one young Indian child named Tamara, but it also describes, without blinders, the horrible injustice that American Indians have faced and the resulting deplorable conditions on too many Indian reservations that must be addressed.

The treatment of Native Americans over two centuries has been a shameful chapter of American life.

It is an incontrovertible fact that the Native Americans were here first. It's also a fact that over the centuries, too many of our government policies dealing with Native Americans have been breathtakingly dishonest. The cheating, the stealing, the racism, and the lies that victimized American Indians are well documented in history. But simply acknowledging that sordid history, although laudable, does not right the wrongs that have occurred.

As we contemplate the tentacles of the past that sometimes strangle the future, it's easy for a more prosperous white America to avoid accountability.

"Wasn't that between my ancestors and your ancestors?" a member of the audience said to Joseph Marshall III, a preeminent Lakota author, after a 2008 lecture on the campus of the University of Colorado in Boulder. "Why should I be held responsible for the plight of Native Americans?" the man asked.

"Because you know the story," Marshall said. It's a profound concept. Once we become aware of an injustice, we become obligated to try to fix it. There are many talented and resourceful Native Americans who desperately want the cycle to end. But how will it end? Or is it destined to last forever? What or who will spark the changes that could create a path of greater opportunity for Native Americans and allow them to become full participants in all that America has to offer?

It seems overwhelming at times. Just as Tamara defensively has occasionally chosen to look away from her unhealed scars, so, too, has America. We don't want to face the atrocities and genocide perpetrated for the benefit of white Americans. We don't want to be accountable. But we are. Because we know the story.

"Not having been alive when an injustice was committed seems like very good reason for denying any responsibility," wrote Julian Rieck, a German scholar in a 2014 essay entitled "A History of Responsibilities."

> *But can you reject the burdened legacy of your community in the same way you can turn down inheriting your deceased parent's debt? You have been born into a specific society with all its achievements and atrocities. You enjoy the benefits like education, the infrastructure, the healthcare system, etc. on the one hand. This means you cannot simply ignore your society's evil past on the other hand. Every German must come to terms with Hitler as part of his or her identity, and not just Goethe or Schiller. Australians and U.S. Americans benefit from past acts of dispossession, slavery and forced assimilation.*

In addition to describing the mistreatment of Native Americans, this book will tell inspiring stories about the wonderful work some very special Native American youth are doing to lift others up and provide role models for survival and success.

There is some remarkable wisdom and philosophy to be shared from generations of a culture that revered nature in a way we would do well to emulate, a generous, nonmaterialistic people who believed it was better to give than possess. In responding to our obligations to the Native Americans who were here first, I believe we help ourselves live up to the full promise and potential of America. Because their story is that of too many others in our country, where, despite its first-world wealth, pockets of people live in third-world conditions.

For all of those reasons, I want to tell you Tamara's story and that of her people.

I

The Lost Girl

Tell me a fact and I will learn
Tell me a truth and I will believe
Tell me a story and I will carry it in my heart forever!
—INDIAN PROVERB

I seldom logged on to my Facebook account. For some reason, though—maybe the same angels at work who'd put the Tamara story in front of me in the first place—I did on March 15, 2016, and found six months' worth of friend requests and messages. One leaped out at me. It was from someone named Tamara. I immediately wondered whether this could be a message from the young girl I had met at the Standing Rock Indian Reservation nearly three decades ago.

I responded by asking if by any chance she was from the Standing Rock Indian Reservation, and I asked her the name of her grandfather. She replied that she was from that reservation and gave me the name of her grandfather. That is when I knew: This was the young girl in the photograph!

What I would learn next stunned me.

Decades after the beating she had suffered in the foster home, Tamara was thirty-three years old and homeless in Minneapolis,

Minnesota. She struggled with nightmares and debilitating anxiety.

"I really don't have much memory of my youth," she would later tell me. "Most of it is a blank. My mind seems to have found a way to black out most of the bad things that happened." As a result, the source of her psychic scars remained a mystery. "Why am I sick and homeless?" she wondered. "Why do I have PTSD? What could have happened to me?" She had fleeting visions of a dark room with a crib off to one side. Musty smells.

So she went to the library and used a computer to search for any information that might help her understand her PTSD and what might have happened to her as a young girl.

Her Google search produced a surprising result: She discovered a speech I had given when I was a U.S. senator. In it, I described the serious challenges Native American youth faced with the poverty and violence on some reservations, and while describing those conditions, I also told a story of the abuse and horrific beating a young child named Tamara had suffered in a foster home on the Standing Rock Indian Reservation years ago. The account read to her like it was a horror story about someone else. She couldn't recall any of it.

That discovery is what prompted her to contact me to find out more. She also thanked me for using her story as an example, hoping her experience would help other Native American children get better care.

I opened my desk drawer and looked again at that yellowed newsprint and that photograph, the tear on her cheek. It had been twenty-seven years. She was thirty-three now. Suddenly, she was real again. She had survived. But how?

As we continued to correspond, Tamara described the road

she had traveled during those nearly three decades. A broken, twisted road.

For many years, Tamara was homeless, on the streets, enduring bitter cold in the winter and hunger year-round. She made herself invisible, a slight girl looking for food and refuge. Most people looked away anyway.

"When I was homeless in Minneapolis, some of the time, I would sleep under a bridge," she remembered. Other nights it was in the park or, in the bitterest cold weather, huddled in handicapped (therefore larger) port-a-potties.

"You would meet a lot of different people," she said. "All of them in the same boat. Homeless. I made a few friends there who would protect me."

What else got her through? Pride. Pride and resilience. She had difficulty finding or keeping a job because of her PTSD. At one point, she worked briefly cleaning bathrooms in nightclubs. At another point, she worked a couple of summer months for a carnival helping put up and take down the rides. For two years, she lived on one meal a day. "I could never ask people for money," she said. "I was too proud. I could never sit on a corner and hold up a sign."

Tamara's story could be the story of a hundred or a thousand or five thousand young boys and girls who are the children of the First Americans—homeless, in a way, from the start.

For a myriad of reasons, many of those who live on the Indian reservations have been left behind. The promises offered the First Americans in treaties and agreements were swiftly broken. As broken as the bones and the heart and soul of this young girl.

Unemployment, poverty, rape and child abuse, rampant alcoholism, and teen suicides are part of everyday life—and death—on too many reservations, the kind of thing you would expect to see in a third-world country. But in America?

The lengthy trail of broken promises that were made to Native Americans has led to the burdens and challenges faced by too many Native American communities.

Yes, those living on the reservations are responsible for their own actions, but the external pressures and broken promises that have visited the reservations bear much of the responsibility.

Tamara didn't have anything resembling a normal homelife. For much of her young life, she was shuttled between grandparents and an occasional aunt and uncle. "My parents were alcoholics," she said. "They lost custody of their children because of child neglect stemming from their alcoholism. But there were times when we were sent back to our home only to be taken away again when things became intolerable.

"Sometimes when we were taken away from our home, it was through the legal system. Other times, it was my grandparents who would see that things were bad in our house, and they would just come and get us and take us away to live with them. That cycle continued through the years.

"Living in the house with my mother was very hard. She constantly berated me and attacked me for the least little thing. It seems awful to say, but while I have only limited memories of my childhood, I have no fond memories at all of my on-again/off-again life at home with my parents.

"My grandparents were a godsend for me. They were the only ones who seemed to care what happened to us.

"One of the few positive memories I have of my childhood that makes me smile is a time when I was eight or nine years old and my grandmother would make a dance costume for me and I would go with them to a powwow and dance with the other fancy shawl dancers. I know my grandma didn't have much material with which to make a dress for the dance, but she used whatever materials she had, and when she finished, to me it looked like the most beautiful dress I had ever seen. I went to the powwow in Wakpala with my two other sisters, and I was happy and so proud to be able to dance with the other kids at the powwow.

"It wasn't easy for my grandparents to take us in and provide for us. They never had very much, but they found a way to make it work. They got food from the government commodity program, and they would stretch that through the week. My grandmother would also recycle hand-me-down clothes through the cousins in our family. I wore mostly hand-me-down clothes, and it wasn't unusual to see a younger niece wear a shirt I had worn five years ago.

"I struggled in school because of my PTSD and other problems I suffered because of my injuries, but I graduated from eighth grade at the Pierre Indian Learning Center. I had difficulties completing regular high school, so I enrolled in the Box-elder Job Corps Civilian Conservation Center in South Dakota and graduated from high school while there."

The description Tamara offers of her life as an adolescent on the Indian reservation is not unique or uncommon. There are a number of Indian reservations where the relentless poverty impacts nearly every other aspect of daily living. It's one thing to describe it and quite another thing to live it.

"I ran away from home as a teenager a number of times. On one of those occasions, I was sent to a Fort Yates group home for punishment. When I was released from the group home, I continued an aimless existence, trying to resolve my health issues and trying to find a place to live that had some stability. But a stable, predicable life seemed to be unattainable for me. I was alone a lot, struggling with my emotional health.

"At age twenty, I enrolled in the Job Corps program in South Dakota and studied business technology. But the PTSD that I suffered from made both studying and working very difficult for me. I did graduate from the Job Corps program but was not able to find a job, given my health difficulties.

"I became a wanderer from Timber Lake, South Dakota, to Valley City, North Dakota, to Rapid City, South Dakota, to Wakpala, Standing Rock, and more places in between. I knew I had PTSD that affected much of what I did, and I was struggling to find a purpose to my life."

The fate of too many young children on Indian reservations is often well beyond their ability to alter or influence the direction of their life.

For Tamara, the severe beating she had suffered early in her life and the brutal treatment she said she had faced at the hands of her mother put her on a path that made for a very difficult recovery.

The Relentless Challenge of Poverty

Those circumstances of poverty, hunger, crime, all things that subjected Tamara to a very difficult life, should have the rest of our country hanging its head in shame. We have visited upon the American Indian population a horrible disservice. They have been lied to, cheated, and robbed with little more than broken treaties to show for it. The relentless poverty, the violence, and other difficulties they experience rest very close to the front door of all of us. There are some success stories of Indian communities that have escaped much of the poverty and related problems, but far too many reservations and communities have been profoundly affected.

If you need specifics, take, for example, a snapshot of the Pine Ridge Reservation in South Dakota, a reservation with major challenges. Unemployment hovers around 80 percent (or higher) with a median income of $4,000. (No, the editors haven't missed a zero. Four thousand.) The median household income in America in 2016 was $55,775.

Alcoholism is pandemic on Pine Ridge. Many babies suffer fetal alcohol syndrome, and the infant mortality rate is five times the national average. (Tamara is convinced that her mother's chronic drinking damaged her.) All this despite the fact that the sale and consumption of alcohol is prohibited by tribal law. Liquor stores just one mile beyond the border of the reservation in Nebraska do a booming business.

Teen suicide there is four times the national average. Life expectancy is forty-eight years for men on the Pine Ridge Reservation and fifty-two for women, lower only than that of Haiti. The school dropout rate is over 70 percent, while teacher turnover is eight times that of the national average. Gangs and gang violence permeate the shadows. Law enforcement is outmanned and underfunded.

And so it goes on too many reservations across America. The poverty bleeds out beyond the borders, too, in cases like Tamara's. Each day, good people and good families wage a losing battle against the tide of despair, crime, and dysfunction.

· · ·

It's important to point out that not all reservations have the same challenges as Pine Ridge. Experiences differ in other parts of the country, and they differ in some state-recognized tribes and urban Indian communities as well.

But the challenges confronting Pine Ridge are too common, especially in many tribes in the northern plains. These conditions are the symptoms. The disease itself is complex, and its origin goes back hundreds of years.

You can't look at our history and view the concept of Manifest Destiny as anything but a license for genocide. It's an ancient tactic: Dehumanize your enemy to ease the consciences of those charged with stealing the land and eradicating its inhabitants. Even today, the ignorant, pervasive racism from those who claim "just another drunk Indian" makes it easier to ignore something within our own borders that would have us talking about human rights in another country.

Americans believe this country has most often been a force for good in this world.

Imperfect and clumsy, misguided at times, but the character of this nation is one of ideals, fairness, freedom, and justice for all.

Justice! Ultimately, this is a story—and a test—about social justice for the original Americans. We have to ask ourselves how we can purport to be an international beacon of freedom and justice when at home we have not really provided the First Americans with a seat at the table in our society.

If you can assign a soul to a nation, then the two great blots on the soul of the United States of America are slavery and the genocide of Native Americans. We can study the past and learn from it, but we can only navigate the future. Granted, there has been progress, but not enough. We know well the civil rights struggles, advances, and setbacks of black Americans, and that is still a work in progress, painful and slow, but inching forward.

But the plight of American Indians, the First Americans, has been ignored, at best an afterthought.

Cardinal Roger Mahony said, "Any society, any nation, is judged on the basis of how it treats its weakest members—the last, the least, the littlest."

When we consider those words, it's hard to argue that Native Americans have not suffered more grievously over the course of American history than any other people.

If you can someday, walk the shores of the Missouri River, where Mandan Indian earth lodges once dotted the hills overlooking the river, the aquatic highway that brought explorers and traders—and smallpox. Imagine the thriving agrarian society that once existed here.

Science tells us we are in the midst of the sixth great extinction in half a billion years; this one, if not induced by mankind, has certainly been accelerated by it. We are seemingly a species bent on suicide, and most at risk are the indigenous peoples who see themselves as the spiritual caretakers of the planet. The irony is evident.

There are 562 federally recognized Indian tribes in America. The American Indian Wars ended long ago, but the carnage never stopped. Today, it's less a case of malice than neglect, but the intent matters less than the reality, which is that America's First People remain America's Forgotten People. This speaks to who we are as a nation.

Our people need our help. And in the end, for us there will be, if not absolution, maybe forgiveness, a positive turn of the karmic wheel. Maybe we are also saving ourselves.

Imagine your own child in that photograph of Tamara. Study

that tear. It's like a crystal ball, but cloudy, filled with unknowns. Tamara's future was uncertain, like that of hundreds of other children with horrific stories of their own.

Funny thing about change. We imagine great marches and movements, but it always starts with an idea, a mission. We touch people every day, and when we do so in a positive manner, it reverberates like rings from a pebble in a pond, one person to the next, one generation to another. The hope is Tamara's story will touch you.

Tamara is the pebble. This book is the ripple in the pond.

2

A People Under Siege

Being I am poor and naked, but I am the chief of the nation.
We do not want riches but we do want to train our children
right.
Riches would do us no good. We could not take them with us
to the other world.
We do not want riches. We want peace and love.

—RED CLOUD, OGLALA LAKOTA
SIOUX (1822–1909)

Flight. That was Tamara's answer to the abuse. "All my childhood memories are of abuse," she said. The beatings never really stopped, even when she emerged from the foster home that might have killed her. When she could, she ran. Who wouldn't? "I got very good at running away . . ."

After the horrific beating she suffered in a foster home, she was taken in by her grandparents. Eventually, Tamara said her mother, who had lost custody because of drinking, regained custody. Then she said there was more abuse. The constant shuttling back and forth between parents and grandparents continued.

Tamara was fifteen the first time she ran away from what she describes as a volatile alcoholic mother and a passive alcoholic father. When she had nowhere else to run, she was forced to return to her dysfunctional home on the Standing Rock Indian

Reservation in the Dakotas. "You should have seen what happened to me when I returned home a few weeks later," she said. "I got one of the worst beatings of my life.

"It's so strange when I see mothers interact with love with their children. I see it, and it's still so foreign to me." She hadn't spoken to her mother in nearly a decade, until their paths crossed at a funeral for Tamara's sister.

Common family activities others take for granted were foreign to Tamara. "I have no memories of Christmas except for one thing. I remember a time when I was told it was Christmas and my older sister, who was a favorite of my mom's, she got a lot of presents. But I was given nothing. She got everything she wanted, and I was told there was nothing for me. But beyond that memory, I don't really remember anything about Christmas with my family. I just don't think we paid any attention to holidays like Christmas," she said.

"The first time I felt like I understood how other people felt about and celebrated Christmas was when I was about twenty-two or twenty-three years old. I was living with my boyfriend's family—he is the father of my oldest child. I remember Christmas. They had a tree and presents and everything. That is the first time I had ever thought about or even understood how others celebrated Christmas."

Tamara lived with the family about six months. It was the first time she had lived with love. "There was so much love. It was a revelation to me. There was no one beating you up. There was no yelling. There was affection. Kisses."

She taps long, slender fingers unconsciously as she talks. She's willowy. Her glasses give her face a studious quality that is not misplaced. Throughout her treacherous journey, she's found solace in books and music. She'd like to learn the Japanese language as a result of watching Japanese movies on the internet. She is very smart and quick and at the same time describes her limitations from PTSD as a major problem for her. She also seems directionless.

She describes her estranged mother as emotionally unstable. "I was walking on eggshells 24-7," Tamara said. Physical abuse was relentless. She remembers one incident in particular. She defiantly stood face-to-face with her mother and took blow after blow. "But I refused to go down," Tamara said. "I wasn't going to give her the satisfaction."

Resilience. Therein lies the hope for the First Americans. After decades of physical and cultural genocide, they keep struggling to their feet. The sacred traditions, the wisdom of living in harmony with nature, the reverence for things living now and past—those things have been kept alive. But there's a difference between life support and living, a difference between survival and thriving, and eventually, the lines get blurred.

Tamara was also sexually abused. The first time she was sexually assaulted, she may have been as young as eight. He was a teenager. The timeline is fuzzy. She's suppressed memories. Tamara says that an extended family member was caught in the act of sexually abusing her, but received no punishment because it would have created a huge family scandal at that time; it was kept swept under the rug for a number of years, until Tamara eventually confided in an older sister about the sexual abuse. Tamara said when her mother had found out, she called Tamara a liar and beat her.

"I sometimes wonder why it happened to me. I always tried so hard to be liked; I wonder if I might have sent the wrong signal to the person who assaulted me. I wonder if I could be at fault. I know better than that, but it's hard not to feel like I was guilty of something. Being a victim of sexual assault is such a violent act to live with. It continues to haunt me long after it happened."

Tamara's experience is tragically too common. According to Justice Department statistics, one in three Native American women have been raped or sexually assaulted, more than twice the national average.

The symptoms of this disrupted culture of violence and despair are startling, none more startling than the prevalence of youth suicide.

Youth suicide was once almost unheard of among Native Americans. Culturally, the whole community was invested in their youth. The loss of culture and tradition removed a natural safety net. Suicide among Native Americans is about three times higher than the national average. On some reservations, the figure is ten times the average. Crisis. Epidemic. Both apply.

One cannot look at Indian issues in a vacuum. To understand where we are, we have to understand where the cycle began. In a historical context, America is young, born in tumult, weaned on expansion and discovery, and in some cases, ruthlessness. It's undeniable that the American government sanctioned and perpetuated the genocide and cultural assault on Native Americans. As the dust has begun to clear, we can begin to see the cycles set in motion, and in the case of Native Americans, cycles of dependency, whether it be substance abuse or hand-to-mouth poverty, the symptoms of an ancient culture knocked down and cast adrift.

It's a trail of broken promises to American Indians that guaranteed education, protection under the law, religious freedom, and some financial support. One can argue that the genocide never really stopped; the momentum has continued in indirect forms. Lack of basic necessities shortens life spans and unleashes a profound sense of hopelessness that permeates Indian culture. Children bear the brunt of the misery, and sadly, there is no sense of urgency in the country to do anything about it.

Tamara, who attempted suicide three times—the first time when she was about eighteen, the second at age twenty-eight, and again in 2015, each time with pills—was one of the survivors.

"For the longest time, I was surprised every day that I woke up," she said. "I still feel that way a lot. I have a lot of sad thoughts." Not every child gets out alive.

Tamara described the last time she attempted to take her own life. She said she felt a bit like a backseat driver, along for the ride but unable to steer.

"I was watching myself open a bottle of pills and my mind kept saying, *No, don't do that.* But I was unable to stop myself. I couldn't let go of the bottle of pills. As I swallowed the pills, I thought, *I don't want this.* I really didn't want to do this. But my body seemed helpless to do what my head was telling me. I had poured water in the bathtub and stepped into the tub and began sliding underwater . . . all the while, my subconscious kept saying I really didn't want to do this.

"I woke up in a hospital bed. My boyfriend had stayed over playing video games, and when I didn't come out of the bathroom, he discovered me sliding underwater. He called 911, and I was revived on the way to the hospital.

"I'm embarrassed and sad for what I've done. And yet I keep thinking about the strangeness of not wanting to do something that your body seems intent on doing. For me, the despair and difficulty of trying to make it through every day just became too heavy to handle. It was always about desperation and despair."

Not all are rescued.

On another Indian reservation, one of the faces lost in the

statistics was Avis Little Wind, fourteen, a member of the Spirit Lake Nation, who hanged herself after the suicides of her father and sister. She lay in bed for weeks, mourning, feeling vacant and alone, and nobody, not even her school, missed her. Eventually, she got out of bed and took her own life. When I heard about the death of Avis Little Wind, I traveled to that Indian reservation to try to understand it. I talked to her relatives, her classmates, and the tribal council. How is it that a fourteen-year-old girl is never missed? No one had a good answer.

She, like Tamara, fell through not cracks, crevices . . . canyons . . . immense gaping holes in the system. Avis Little Wind might have survived if she'd had mental health treatment. It wasn't available on that reservation.

Tamara can relate to the sense of abandonment that Avis Little Wind felt, the feeling that there is nowhere to turn. But the anguish isn't always evident on the surface. She says she suffers in silence. "Keeping a mask on is my go-to. I figured out very early in life that all I have, when it really comes down to it, is me, myself, and I."

According to the National Alliance on Mental Illness, almost 90 percent of suicides can be attributed to mental health issues that are often treatable. Suicide is linked to poverty, unemployment, depression, and substance abuse. Ironically, the poverty that is a contributing factor to mental health issues is also a barrier to treatment, especially in rural areas, where most reservations are located.

The Indian Health Service system serves two million American Indians in thirty-five states, and the funding for the IHS is far short of that which is needed to serve the Indian people.

A 2009 Associated Press story adds, "The U.S. has an obligation, based on a 1787 agreement between tribes and the government, to provide American Indians with free health care on reservations. But that promise has not been kept. About one-third more is spent per capita on health care for felons in federal prison than is spent per capita for Indian health care according to 2005 data from the health service."

According to Indian Health Services, alcoholism is six times the national average on reservations. Tamara feels that she and the three siblings born after her may be subject to varying degrees of fetal alcohol syndrome.

Many of the issues Indians face today were previously rare in the culture. In 1903, in Canton, South Dakota, what was called the Canton Asylum for Insane Indians opened, but government officials were puzzled in the beginning by the lack of patients.

"Where are all the crazy Indians?" one official is said to have asked.

"We don't have any," was the response.

"Well, get some," the official replied.

And so the institution became a prison for alcoholics or those who opposed government policy or business interests. An investigation in 1927 by the Bureau of Indian Affairs discovered that a large number of patients showed no indications of mental illness. More than 350 Indians were kept there in deplorable conditions. At least 121 died before the place was shuttered in 1934.

Hope4Alaska

The health care challenges and teen suicide tragedies are difficult stories to tell, but there is also hope and inspiration in the work being done by other Native American and Alaskan Native youth who are working to end the scourge of teen suicide. One of those is a remarkable young Native Alaskan woman named Teresa "Tessa" Baldwin.

Raised in a small Native Alaskan community just thirty miles from the arctic circle, Tessa was the second of eight children. She credits her teachers at a boarding school she attended for giving her the confidence to succeed. They kept telling her, "You're going to do it," and she became a believer that she could and would succeed. She would put that confidence to good use.

She was a high school sophomore when a close friend and classmate took her own life just as, when she was five, her favorite uncle had taken his. Tessa decided that day that someone needed to say something or do something about the number of suicides that were rampant in the Native Alaska population. She felt there needed to be a dialogue about a subject that no one seemed to want to talk about.

"The elders among our Native population did not want public discussion of the issue of teen suicide," she said. "They felt that talking about suicide reflected poorly on Native Alaskans, and such a public discussion could provide ideas for other youth to consider suicide."

But Tessa was not willing to walk away from a conversation she felt that Native Alaskans needed to have about the previously taboo subject of teen suicide.

That determination of a sixteen-year-old girl resulted in the creation of an organization dedicated to calling attention to and finding solutions to the teen suicide crisis.

"I started this organization alone one day while I was on Facebook, and the name *Hope4Alaska* just popped into my mind. It became something I worked on throughout the rest of my school years," she said. "I had a lot of support from individual students and student groups, including writing grants and developing ideas for funding our project. I'm proud that ours was a completely youth-driven project."

Tessa began to do school convocations on the subject. She traveled to over thirty counties in Alaska doing presentations to groups of students on the subject of suicide prevention. In each school, she not only began the dialogue but also created projects each school could use to address the problems of teen suicide.

"I kept track of the number of tragic stories I heard from my visits to the Alaska schools, and there were over two hundred personal stories told to me about teen suicides," she said. "There were tons of very personal stories that brought a lot of tears to my eyes, and it kept reminding me the importance of what I was doing."

Following her high school graduation, Tessa went to college in San Diego and from there enrolled at Columbia University in New York City to obtain a master's degree in social work. As this book was being completed, Tessa was in her last year at Columbia and was planning to go back to Alaska to embark on a career in mental health. She's already a leader. She has the potential to do much more for the next generations of her people.

Turning the Tide of Despair

One day, the work done by people like Tessa Baldwin will begin turning despair into hope for all Native American youth and end the scourge of teen suicide.

We could do more to stop that despair from ever taking hold.

As a nation, we tend to be reactive. We don't like to think of what might happen. We hope for the best and ignore the worst. When it comes to floods, for instance, we put most of our money into cleaning up after one, but the money would be better spent

upstream before the flood happens. Actual flood control requires investment in the environment, managing watersheds,
minimizing runoff, strategic placement of dams, and the construction of dikes. It saves lives and it saves money.

So, too, can we mitigate the flood of despair with wiser investments in Indian reservations, where 22 percent of Native
Americans live, starting with finding ways to keep fractured families together.

What most Americans consider necessities are luxuries there.
A full 28 percent of homes on the reservation don't have adequate
plumbing or kitchen facilities compared to 5.4 percent nationally.

U.S. News & World Report said in 2014 that more than one
in four Native people live in poverty. "At 11 percent, the native
unemployment rate in the third quarter of 2014 was almost double the national rate of 6.2 percent." The year that President
Barack Obama visited the Standing Rock Indian Reservation, the
unemployment rate there stood at more than 60 percent.

As a result, the disintegration of a family often begins with
good intentions: with parents doing what is necessary to provide
for their children, and that means finding employment off the
reservation.

That parental distance makes it harder to hold the family together. In many cases, unsupervised children get into trouble.
That results in the parents replaced by foster parents, who in some
cases see children as a source of income. Tamara's grandfather,
in fact, believed that chronic high unemployment on the reservation resulted in children being seized and sold into involun-
tary servitude for a monthly check. And so the cycle begins again.

In South Dakota, Indian children comprise just 15 percent
of the child population yet account for more than half the children in foster care, many of them being removed from their cul-

ture. Nearly seven hundred Indian children each year are removed from their homes.

In the late 1960s and early 1970s, the Association on American Indian Affairs found that in states with high Native American populations, as many as 25–35 percent of Indian children were being removed from their homes. South Dakota senator James Abourzek responded by sponsoring legislation to address that issue.

The 1978 Indian Child Welfare Act mandates, with the exception of extenuating circumstances, that Native American children be placed with relatives, a tribal member, or a Native American family, but in many cases, that isn't happening. In South Dakota, Indian foster homes are in short supply, so most end up removed from their cultural identity, their spiritual center.

A common view from tribal members is that children are sometimes taken from homes by inexperienced social workers making arbitrary decisions that don't take into consideration cultural differences. For example, in 2011, only 6 percent of social workers in South Dakota were Native Americans.

Others point to a system that rewards the state with federal dollars going straight to the Department of Social Services in a given state for each foster child placed. "They make a living off of our children," Juanita Sherick, a tribal social worker for the Pine Ridge Reservation in South Dakota, once told NPR.

"Cousins are disappearing; family members are disappearing," added Peter Lengkeek, a Crow Creek Tribal Council member in South Dakota. "It's kidnapping. That's how we see it."

According to Health and Human Services statistics, the rate of Native American children's removal from their families rose from 1.5 times the rate of the general population in 2000 to 2.7 in 2014. Among African Americans, that rate was reduced in the same time frame from 2.5 to 1.8 times the rate of the rest of the population.

What's happening to Native Americans is undeniable. Is it intentional government policy? Is malevolence at work here? It's a hard case to make. Another explanation is that even as we try to understand the generational cycles of poverty and cultural alienation that have brought Native Americans to this tragic juncture, we must, too, recognize the often unintended consequences of bureaucratic cycles and malaise.

There are obvious cases where intervention is critical to a child's safety, but the cultural divide between whites and Indians is a large one. Agents charged with helping and protecting Native Americans are often not knowledgeable enough from a cultural standpoint to do so effectively.

There have been many Indian success stories—perhaps some better labeled *survival stories*—and it is clear that many members of the white establishment meant well, but we needn't go too far down that paved path to see that even in the absence of malice, one result of failed government policy is that American Indians' life expectancy across all reservations is 4.4 years less than the rest of the U.S. population.

Much of that may be due to the siege on indigenous culture, whether it be intentional or accidental. The traditions and values may survive but, in many cases, without the means to fully employ them. When you're just surviving, you're not really living. Things break down. How could they not when a culture is effectively uprooted and interred? One term is commonly used as a description of this phenomenon: *historical trauma*.

The process of the near extinction for the Mandan Indians, which began with smallpox epidemics in the 1830s, ended in December of 2016 with the death of Edwin Benson on the Fort

Berthold Indian Reservation. He was the last person alive who could fluently speak Mandan, or Nu'eta, as it is properly called. When he died, Three Affiliated Tribes councilman Cory Spotted Bear told journalist Lauren Donovan of *The Bismarck Tribune,* "The world we live in becomes less."

The siege continues.

3

The Kindness of a Stranger

The United States, which would live on Christian principles with all of the peoples of the world, cannot omit a fair deal for its own Indian citizens.

—HARRY TRUMAN

In Minneapolis, after nearly eight years of couch surfing and homelessness, as she described it, Tamara was battling with emotional difficulties and struggling to earn just a little bit of money in several temporary jobs that she had trouble continuing because of her PTSD and other issues.

Then two people she didn't know changed her life for the better.

The first was Ronald Russell, a middle-aged man who, in most circumstances, you wouldn't expect to come into contact with someone like Tamara. Except that Ronald was a caring and religious man who always looked for ways to provide blessings for people who were struggling.

He was an active member of a church that had a mission finding ways to help the homeless. As he worked in various jobs in the Twin Cities, he made a conscious effort to reach out to those he saw on the streets who needed help.

Ronald was working as an Uber driver and was also working

with a nightclub in Minneapolis called Seven to supervise bathroom attendants for their customers. One day while driving in downtown Minneapolis, he saw Tamara and several others who appeared homeless spending time near the entrance to a vacant building. He stopped to visit with them to see if he could do anything for them, and during the conversation, he asked Tamara if she was interested in a part-time job.

"I usually stopped to talk when I encountered those who were homeless to see if there was any way I could be helpful to them," Ronald said. "My priority was to offer a blessing to those who were having a hard time. Because of my work with the church, I knew the location of most of the shelters and feeding programs where those who were homeless might find the comfort of a hot meal or a safe place to sleep.

"Tamara was one of those I had seen a number of times on the street, and when I asked her if she would like to have a part-time job as a bathroom attendant at a Minneapolis club, she seemed excited by the opportunity to get a job and earn a little money.

"I had occasionally helped other homeless people find some odd jobs, and I knew the difficulties they confronted in making a transition from being on the streets to working at a job. Not everyone can do it, and some don't want to try.

"Most people don't understand the issues people face when they find a way to move from homelessness to a job. Just knowing the right clothes to wear, when to be at work, what is expected of you, that's not easy. The basics of being presentable and finding a place to clean up or shower before work . . . these are things that are hard for those who are homeless but trying to get a job and find a place to live.

"When Tamara told me she was willing to take the job, I

drove her to a thrift store and purchased some clothes for her so she would have something to wear that was appropriate for the job. I had done that for several others who were in transition from the streets to a job.

"About a week after we discussed the job, Tamara started work at the nightclub in the evenings. She proved to be a conscientious worker and did a very good job during the couple of months she worked at the nightclub.

"Her job was to organize the counter in front of the bathroom mirror in the women's bathroom and set out items like candy, gum, cologne, and cigarettes for the women who used the restroom. She also had the responsibility to keep the restroom clean. That meant performing some less appealing jobs like cleaning up after people who were getting sick and throwing up in a toilet or sink. Still, she seemed to enjoy the opportunity to earn a salary as well as the tips that people gave to the attendant. The job didn't pay much, but with the tips she earned, Tamara finally had some money of her own."

Ronald said, "She was hard to get close to. She was quiet and reserved, and there always seemed to be an edge or a guarded sense that someone might be trying to take advantage of her or hurt her.

"One night as Tamara was working at the nightclub, it was getting very late at night, and I didn't think it was safe for her to be walking alone on the streets of Minneapolis that late, so I offered to give her a ride home. Tamara declined the offer and said she would be fine."

Tamara later revealed why she didn't want a ride home that night.

"I turned him down because I didn't want him or any others I worked with to know I was sleeping under a bridge in downtown Minneapolis," she said. "I was embarrassed to admit that I had no other place to go except to share a space under a bridge with others who were homeless.

"But Ronald kept insisting. He told me that he was not comfortable letting me walk alone downtown at that hour. I finally relented, and I got in his car thinking I could just have him drop me off some blocks away from downtown. As he began to drive away from the club, he asked where I was staying. I told him just to drop me off on the edge of downtown.

"'I'm not going to do that,' he said. 'Let me know where you live, and I'll take you there.'

"After some discussion back and forth, I finally admitted I didn't have a place to live and that I was sleeping under a bridge. He was surprised by that, but without hesitating, he said, 'I'm not going to drive you to the bridge. I am going to drive you to the Salvation Army where you can be safe and you will find a place to sleep.'

"'Well, I'm not going to the Salvation Army,' I said.

"But he was already driving in that direction. As he pulled up in front of the Salvation Army building, it was late at night, and I told him again I was not going to go into the Salvation Army.

"He said, 'Well, then, it's going to be a long night, because my car is not moving from this spot until I see you get out of the car and walk through that front door.'

"I could tell he was not going to relent, and so I finally and grudgingly decided I would walk into the Salvation Army.

"I remember walking up to the door of that building thinking that it was interesting that the location of the Salvation Army was only a couple of blocks from the bridge where I had been sleeping. I thought of the others who were sleeping under the bridge that night.

"A lot has happened to me since I opened the door and walked into the Salvation Army. And if I were to see Ronald Russell again, I would tell him his insistence that I go to the Salvation Army was the turning point for me. I was stubborn and frightened about going there. I knew how to survive on the streets, but to me, the Salvation Army was a strange place, and I had no idea what to expect.

"But that walk from his car to the door of the Salvation Army turned out to be a journey that could have saved my life. It led to some positive changes in my life, getting me off the streets and out of immediate danger. It didn't happen quickly. I ended up staying there for nearly a year and a half. But through it all, I began getting the help I needed to get back on my feet.

"My work at the nightclub was very short term, and I don't think I ever really had the opportunity to thank Ronald Russell, but I believe he must have known that the Salvation Army would be the type of place that could change my life. The kindness of someone who barely knew me is something I will never forget."

Addressing Homelessness in Indian Country

Tamara was one of an estimated six hundred thousand homeless people in America, according to the U.S. Department of Housing and Urban Development. That would be like putting the entire city of Milwaukee on the streets.

While no demographic has suffered historically as much as Native Americans in the United States, parallels can be found in the suffering of the homeless, who have become a permanent underclass in recent times, not despite Wall Street booming but because of it. The disparity of wealth in America has never been greater. The top 1 percent owns 40 percent of the wealth. The top 20 percent owns 90 percent of it. The homeless own next to 0 percent.

This disparity is political, it's class warfare, and it's short-sighted. Monied interests have always reviled the social safety net programs instituted by Franklin Roosevelt during the Great Depression, but some of them can be credited with creating the prosperity of the 1950s. Because when our country invests in its people, those investments pay off.

Investments—following through on promises made—would benefit the whole of America from reservation to inner city today. The current imbalance actually hurts the economy. The Organisation for Economic Co-operation and Development said in a 2015 report, "Beyond its impact on social cohesion, growing inequality is harmful for long-term economic growth. The rise of income inequality from 1985 and 2005, for example, is estimated to have knocked 4.7 percentage points off cumulative growth between 1990 and 2010."

When the economy is manipulated by already powerful interests that shift more and more wealth to the top, the weight of debt forced upon those on the bottom facing stagnant wages and increasing costs of living and education makes it difficult to share in and to invest in the American dream.

My book *Take This Job and Ship It* illustrates how American companies are rewarded with tax breaks for shipping jobs and parking profits overseas, thereby undermining the national tax base and labor force through what is essentially subsidized labor—a double whammy for working American families who get paid less and absorb more of the societal burdens.

This is economic cannibalism, by which manufacturers en masse suppress the wages in the very same marketplace in which they intend to market products. The result is inevitable debt on American families, and indebtedness can quite literally be economic slavery. Plus, it's bad for business to have customers who can't afford their products. The poor get poorer, and the poorest among us, including those on reservations, quite literally die.

We have the wealth in our country to accomplish great things and allow more people to share in our largesse while maintaining competitive and innovative ideals. President Trump told American workers in 2017, "The system is rigged." Then he rigged it some more with a gigantic tax cut that greatly favored the wealthiest among us—corporate welfare—laying the groundwork for more national debt and foreshadowing the inevitable "necessary" cuts to social safety net programs to those who can least afford them, such as many of those who blithely voted for Trump.

And the beat goes on.

In his State of the Union address in 1944, Franklin Roosevelt talked about a second Bill of Rights that included the "right of every American to a decent home." Lyndon Baines Johnson carried the torch when he declared a war on poverty.

President Ronald Reagan took a different approach. His policies were close to declaring a war on the impoverished. He used a national recession as the excuse to slash federal spending on subsidized housing; Reagan cut funding from $26 billion to $8 billion, a trend that continued. By the time George W. Bush took office, the Department of Housing and Urban Development budget had been cut 60 percent. Reagan, who famously couldn't even recognize his HUD secretary, also presided over a scandal in which HUD funding was diverted from building and sustaining housing for the poor to Republican consultants. The swamp had not yet been drained.

Inevitably, when such programs are cut, the most vulnerable among us are most affected. Lacking the intellectual curiosity to understand how people like Tamara end up on the streets, many often resort to demonizing them.

Reagan's attitude was crystalized after his reelection in 1984. Forty years after FDR set the goal to house all Americans adequately, President Reagan victimized the victims when he said blithely, "The people who are sleeping on the grates . . . the homeless . . . are homeless, you might say, by choice." Yeah, and ketchup is a vegetable.

Tamara's choices were decidedly limited. She couch surfed when she could, lived under a bridge and lived on the streets when she couldn't. Every winter, in cities across the north, the homeless huddle in freezing conditions. Some never wake up.

In 2016, forty-three Minnesotans froze to death, most on the streets of Minneapolis, because they couldn't find adequate shelter. This in a supposedly progressive city that found the money to subsidize gleaming new baseball and football stadiums.

There's a cost to homelessness that goes beyond the human misery. According to HUD, the annual cost per homeless person is $30,000–$50,000, mostly due to the financial impact of providing emergency medical services or housing of a different sort—jails. That's more than the $32,000 a year it costs to house a federal prisoner, according to 2015 statistics from the Federal Bureau of Prisons.

It would simply be far cheaper to get the homeless off the streets and create the modicum of stability that is the first step to employment and reintroduction into mainstream society. And the strategy works. By 2015, a decade after implementing its Housing First project, Utah reduced its chronic homelessness by 91 percent.

This shouldn't be framed as a liberal or conservative argument. Ultimately, we all want results. A conservative named Tom Pendleton helped create the original pilot project in Salt Lake City that housed seventeen of the most challenging cases, the success of which proved to be a model for the rest of the state and for the country. Other communities have embraced the proactive approach but are studying the Utah model to see what they've done that has worked so well.

Pendleton wasn't an easy convert. "Because I was raised as a cowboy in the west desert," he said in an interview with NPR, "and I have said over the years, 'You lazy bums, get a job, pull yourself up by the bootstraps.'"

It takes leadership—people with an open mind and a vision like Tom Pendleton. Because Utah is a state with a smaller population, there's more intimate communication between advocates and agencies. The Church of Jesus Christ of Latter-day Saints has been a key supporter as well. In short, the community—government on one end, activists on the other, with excellent communication—worked together to improve lives and improve their communities. Caseworkers are judicious when it comes to placing homeless people in apartments. They are vetted; if someone is known to be dealing drugs, it's not going to work.

When we look at Tamara's case, we see a foster care system in which her caseworker was swamped in cases. The home in which Tamara was so awfully beaten as a toddler couldn't have been properly vetted. Now, imagine if social services had been properly funded. Tamara would have stood a much better chance of emerging as a productive member of society without those burdens.

Looking back at the housing cuts that began under Reagan, the net drain on society is unfathomable. All political philosophies have arguable pros and cons, but they all fail when they ignore basic human needs and basic human decency: the means to pursue happiness, as it were.

Historically, there have always been surges of homelessness in America driven by social and economic upheaval and by changes in technology. There were wandering agricultural workers during the Revolutionary War.

Chris Roberts, who wrote a report on the subject for *SF Weekly* in 2015, entitled "The Great Eliminator: How Ronald Reagan Made Homelessness Permanent," said, "Almost always, it [homelessness] was temporary. As soon as the economy recovered, homeless people recovered, too. They went back inside and resumed normal lives. In the meantime, there was a safety net." This time, the economic stratification and cycle of poverty seems more permanent.

Peter Dreier, an urban policy analyst and the director of the Urban & Environmental Policy department at Occidental College in Los Angeles, said, "Every park bench in America—everywhere a homeless person sleeps—should have Ronald Reagan's name on it."

Intergenerational Trauma

Because America is a melting pot, the issues of disparity and homelessness, as Roberts noted, have largely been driven by social and economic events. Through immigration, we've formed a unique homogenized society with fewer generational cultural roots. Cultural continuity was more often a personal decision.

There are two prominent exceptions—the obvious cultural trauma and cyclical poverty-related ramifications endured by African Americans whose ancestors were brought as slaves to

America four hundred years ago and then, of course, the First Americans, who faced a policy of extermination.

Too strong a word, *extermination*? No.

Thomas Jefferson said in 1813, "This unfortunate race, whom we had been taking so much pains to save and to civilize, have by their unexpected desertion and ferocious barbarities justified extermination and now await our decision on their fate."

Today, like a stick in the eye of Native Americans who were forced to surrender the Black Hills decades later under the relentless march of settlers and gold prospectors, Thomas Jefferson's face is carved into a granite mountain in South Dakota in those very same Black Hills. Yes, he was a great president. But one with a blind eye to the obligations we owe to Native Americans.

What James Monroe wrote in a letter to Andrew Jackson in 1817 is especially telling: "The hunter or savage state requires a greater extent of territory to sustain it, than is compatible with the progress and just claims of civilized life, and must yield to it. Nothing is more certain, than, if the Indian tribes do not abandon that state, and become civilized, that they will decline, and become extinct. The hunter state, tho maintain'd by warlike spirits, presents but a feeble resistance to the more dense, compact, and powerful population of civilized man."

It is important to understand the role that the cultural trauma from the history of the mistreatment of American Indians plays in the lives of Native American youth today.

According to an Annie E. Casey Foundation report, "When compared to kids from other racial and ethnic groups—American Indian children are least likely to graduate high school on time, be connected to school or work as young adults, or earn an associate degree or higher. More than half of American Indian children live in high poverty neighborhoods and 62 percent live in low-income families, according to the publication. American Indian kids scored just 413 out of 1,000 in [the] report's Race for Results index, which compares how children are progressing on key milestones across racial and ethnic groups at the national and state levels. Only African-American children fared worse, earning a score of 369."

For the present to have relevance, the past must be revisited. It is a major part of what is called *cultural trauma*. Where have we been, where are we now, and where are we going?

The disgrace of what is called the Trail of Tears is a good place to start. It is a trail that leads to the present, and to the tear captured forever, suspended in time, in the photograph of Tamara, then just a young child, cowering in the dark, perhaps irrecoverably damaged.

The past reminds us of the sometimes frail and unjust nature of laws—legal justification for inhumanity. In 1830, two years after gold was discovered in Georgia, the Indian Removal Act legitimized the forced exile of the Muskogee, Seminole, Chickasaw, Choctaw, and Cherokee nations, including freed black slaves who lived among them, from ancestral lands in the southeastern part of America, to unfamiliar land west of the Mississippi River. The resulting forced march of the Trail of Tears in 1838 claimed some eight thousand Cherokee lives—maybe more.

"I saw the helpless Cherokees arrested and dragged from their homes, and driven at the bayonet point into the stockades. And in the chill of a drizzling rain on an October morning I saw them loaded like cattle or sheep into six hundred and forty-five wagons and started toward the west," wrote Private John G. Burnett. "On the morning of November the 17th we encountered a terrific sleet and snow storm with freezing temperatures and from that day until we reached the end of the fateful journey on

March the 26th 1839, the sufferings of the Cherokees were awful. The trail of the exiles was a trail of death. They had to sleep
in the wagons and on the ground without fire. And I have
known as many as twenty-two of them to die in one night of
pneumonia due to ill treatment, cold and exposure."

In 1874, when an expedition led by General George Armstrong Custer discovered gold in the Black Hills, the empty
promises of the Fort Laramie Treaty were laid bare. That treaty
gave ownership of the Black Hills to the Sioux, and the treaty
provisions were soon violated by the government seizing ownership of the Black Hills. History was repeated.

The North American Indian population fell from an estimated twelve million in the year 1500 to fewer than a quarter
million by 1900. It's hard to argue that the survivors have been
little more than an afterthought in public policy when one ex-
amines the state of American Indians in the United States.

Still, as hard as people tried over the years to force assimilation on Native Americans in the arrogant belief that Western
civilization was superior in all things, traditionalists have kept
their history, spirituality, and culture alive. And therein lie the
seeds of hope for the recovery of the culture.

Luther Standing Bear, an Oglala Lakota chief and author,
once spoke to the presumption of Western values: "I am going
to venture that the man who sat on the ground in his tipi medi-
tating on life and its meaning, accepting the kinship of all crea-
tures, and acknowledging unity with the universe of things was
infusing into his being the true essence of civilization."

A smug journalist once asked Gandhi, "What do you think
of Western civilization?" Gandhi replied, "I think it would be a
good idea." That pithy comment reveals a truism prevalent about
America—a certainty that our materialistic Judeo-Christian

mores are superior. But certainty in one's own moral superiority is a particular kind of blindness.

Conservative icon Ayn Rand, for whom selfishness was the highest virtue, epitomized that mind-set. "Let's suppose they were all beautifully innocent savages, which they certainly were not," Rand said in 1974. "What was it that they were fighting for, if they opposed white men on this continent? For their wish to continue a primitive existence, their right to keep part of the earth untouched, unused, and not even as property, but just keep everybody out so that you will live practically like an animal? Any white person who brings the elements of civilization had the right to take over this continent . . ."

Manifest Destiny was the policy of the U.S. government. It was grounded in a belief that the United States was "destined, divinely ordained" to control an arbitrary swath of what they called North America. And yet, when one considers the state of affairs driven by that smug surety, especially when we look at the havoc wreaked on some parts of Mother Earth by our industrialization, it's hard to argue against Native American wisdom. David Ipina, a member of the Yurok tribe, said, "Mother Earth is not a resource, she is an heirloom."

Our reflection on this country's history cannot avoid the harsh reality that might is not necessarily accompanied by morality. Compared to European nations, ours is a young country. As time unfolds, we see the patterns and continuation of cycles caused by slavery and wholesale genocide. Poverty and disenfranchisement beget more of the same.

A quote sometimes attributed to Albert Einstein states, "The definition of insanity is doing the same thing over and over again but expecting different results." That quote applies to many aspects of life in Indian country, from a dysfunctional bureaucracy to a general malaise. On an individual basis with Tamara, we can see how a ponderous, entrenched bureaucracy can lead to horrific outcomes. An overhaul is in order.

The trick is in the balance for Native Americans—living in today's world while holding on to cultural wisdom. David Swallow Jr., a Lakota leader, said, "The time for handouts is gone. We don't want or need charity, yet the poverty must end. We need to stop the mismanaged handouts from the government and step up into a position of taking charge of our own lives . . . We need business education, and we need jobs. We need workshops to teach us how to create and run our own businesses."

The housing experiment in Salt Lake City proved to be an investment that paid off. The key word to keep in mind is *investment*. You plant the seeds, care for them, and they grow.

Tamara's homelessness, on the other hand, was a continuation of a centuries-old cycle that began when Native Americans were driven from their ancestral homes. So many promises have been broken along the way. Always, capitalism—if not theft—trumped human rights and morality. We've salted their ground instead of seeding it.

Driven from Their Ancestral Homes

In 1787, Congress enacted the Northwest Ordinance, which created the Northwest Territories. It included Article III about Indians, which stated the following: "The utmost good faith shall always be observed towards the Indians; their lands and property shall never be taken from them without their consent; and, in their property, rights and liberty, they shall never be invaded or disturbed unless in just and lawful wars authorized by Congress; but law founded in justice and humanity, shall from time to time be made for preventing wrongs being done to them and for preserving peace and friendship with them."

Notwithstanding that commitment, the relentless movement by non-Indians into Indian lands beginning in the early years of our country continued to stoke unrest between the Indian tribes and those who were encroaching on land that belonged to them. As that encroachment continued, the Indians resisted and took aggressive action to protect their property and themselves. Eventually, the government began deploying the military to protect those who were encroaching.

By 1830, there were five Indian tribes in the eastern part of the United States that were described by non-Indians as "civilized tribes"—the Cherokee, Choctaw, Muscogee, Chickasaw, and the Seminole tribes. Civilized or not, the white settlers had their eyes on land that belonged to those tribes, and they pressed the government to seize some of that Indian land to make more property available for non-Indians.

Bribes and threats were routinely used to persuade Indians to sign away their rights to tribal lands. When that didn't work, brute force was also used against the Indians. The treatment of American Indians was one of lies, deception, and fraud and the use of the military to support that fraud. As the nature of our young country took shape, the government made some dreadful and deadly decisions about how to deal with American Indians.

The discovery of gold in Georgia led to speculators pushing to take away the land belonging to the tribes. That continuing pressure by non-Indians to remove the tribes to areas west of the Mississippi River eventually led to the passage of the Indian Removal Act of 1830. In that legislation, which passed the U.S. Senate by only one vote, Congress gave the president the authority to force the removal of the tribes. President Andrew Jackson in 1830 supported and pushed for that legislation and took the first steps under the legislation to take the Indian land and force the removal of the indigenous people.

When Jackson ordered the Indian tribes' removal, he said it would "enable them to pursue happiness in their own way and under their own rude institutions . . . to cast off their savage habits and become an interesting, civilized and Christian community."

A special, permanent stain will always be reserved for President Jackson and others who participated in the removal of the Indian tribes from the eastern and southern states. Society's evolution is far from complete. How sad in 2017, that President Trump cluelessly "honored" Navaho Code Talkers who helped America win World War II, before a portrait of Jackson, a man who practiced genocide. Trump then used the ceremony as a platform to attack a political opponent, Elizabeth Warren, derisively calling her "Pocahontas," a reference to her having an Indian ancestor.

The Indian Removal Act and the resulting Trail of Tears remains a stain on the soul of our country. There is simply no way to accept or justify the way the First Americans were treated by those who arrived later. It is a reminder that what is law is not always moral. But in many ways, the Removal Act was just the beginning of the difficulties faced by Indian tribes.

Those who survived the forced march lived to see the same history played out again on the Great Plains several decades later. The treaties signed with the plains Indians were also promptly violated by encroaching prospectors and other non-Indians.

While history books chronicle the Civil War of the 1860s when the North and the South were at war, there is scarce mention of the American Indian Wars during which the U.S. cavalry relentlessly attacked the men, women, and children of Indian tribes.

As always, imbalance and inequity breeds conflict. The Dakota Sioux of Minnesota had seen thirty million acres of their land taken from them. They were living on much smaller reservations and were short of food, and many were starving. Predictably, they lashed out at the white settlers who were beneficiaries of the land the tribes had lost. The resulting battles were known as the Minnesota Uprising. More than seven hundred men, women, and children, whites and Indians, died in the 1862 revolt.

It's paradoxical that while Abraham Lincoln, another face carved on Mount Rushmore, was leading a fight against slavery in the South, his soldiers were simultaneously leading an Indian eradication program on the Great Plains, where Tamara's ancestors lived. One man's liberator can be another's master.

General John Pope, who is better known for his defeats at the first and second Battles of Bull Run in Virginia, was sent to quell the rebellion. He said, "It is my purpose utterly to exterminate the Sioux if I have the power to do so."

Indians implicated in the uprising were brought to trial. On December 26, 1862, the day after Christmas, in the largest mass execution in American history, thirty-eight Dakota Indians were hung from the gallows in Mankato, Minnesota. Some may find solace in the fact that Lincoln commuted the sentences of 265 Indians, a very unpopular political move, but the Dakota Sioux have always been convinced that the trials were a sham and many of those hanged had nothing to do with the uprising.

The cycle of attacks and retribution continued. The confrontations between the Indians and the cavalry continued with greater intensity in Minnesota, the Dakotas, and adjoining Great

Plains states. Killing led to more killing, and the American Indian Wars of the Great Plains spread while the attention of the country was focused on the Civil War back east.

Meanwhile, in the Dakotas, places like Whitestone Hill, Killdeer Mountain, Rainy Butte, and many more became killing grounds. On September 3, 1863, General Alfred Sully's troops attacked a large encampment of Yanktonai, Dakota, Hunkpapa Lakota, and Blackfeet Indians at Whitestone Hill in south-central North Dakota, the intent being punishment for the Dakota Conflict of 1862, although history suggests that the victims of the attack had not been involved in the related Minnesota Uprising.

Hundreds of Indians were slaughtered at Whitestone Battlefield. But with winter approaching, the devastating loss of their material possessions, tepees, and tools, and all the buffalo meat, which was burned until tallow ran in a river down the hill, the Indians were left nearly destitute for the coming winter. More would die in the harsh Dakota winter to come.

The tactics were abhorrent. Harkening back to 1838, when smallpox-infected blankets were used to nearly wipe out the Mandan, after one battle in 1864 near what is now Rhame, North Dakota, Captain James L. Fisk, leader of a government expedition to protect immigrants, left behind hardtack that was laced with strychnine, resulting in the death of many hungry Indians who ate it. In Captain Fisk's writings, he was unapologetic. The occupation of Native American lands continued as Indians were subjugated or exterminated.

The original Treaty of Fort Laramie in 1851 and the second Fort Laramie Treaty in 1868 were designed to calm the wars on the prairies by setting aside a vast portion of land for Indians. Instead, they proved to be documented broken promises. Among other things, the treaties set aside lands that belonged to the Indians that were not to be encroached upon by white settlers. Those lands included the sacred Black Hills of what is now South Dakota.

However, the discovery of gold in the Black Hills in 1874 changed everything. The rush to the Black Hills by prospectors and others who were following the gold rush overwhelmed the Indians. The U.S. government did little to stop the violation of the treaty provisions, and the Black Hills began giving up its gold that could be used to finance the Civil War going on out east. It is estimated that over $1 billion in gold was removed from the Black Hills.

Article VI of the U.S. Constitution says that "treaties are the supreme law of the land," but the track record of the U.S. government, when it comes to honoring treaties with Native Americans, is abysmal. How could resentment and distrust not follow?

Leaders like Sitting Bull and Crazy Horse fought back. They held the moral high ground but lost the land they had once freely roamed.

Attempts to assimilate uprooted tribes perpetuated the attack on Indian sovereignty. In 1887, President Grover Cleveland signed into law the Dawes Severalty Act to devastating effect on the already besieged culture of Native Americans.

The act divided reservations held communally among tribal members. The goal was to create a self-sufficient agrarian culture and to end what would be today called "welfare handouts" by some. Native American families received 160 acres, but there were strings attached—before any family could sell their allotment, if they so chose, they were required to get a certificate of competency. Lacking that, the land reverted to the federal government for sale, usually to white settlers. Franklin Delano Roosevelt finally abolished the act in 1934. By then, the Dawes

Act had decimated Indian landholdings from 138 million
acres in 1887 to 78 million by 1900.

The Cost of Harnessing the Missouri River

The mismanagement did not end there. In the 1950s, the federal
government, to stop the chronic flooding of the Missouri River
and provide for irrigation and navigation benefits on the river,
proposed to build a series of main-stem dams. Those large dams
required the flooding of prime Indian lands on a number of Indian reservations. On the Fort Berthold Indian Reservation, the
prime bottomland where the Indians produced fruits and berries was permanently flooded with water.

There can be little argument that "the deal" to build the dams
was virtually forced upon the tribes by the federal government.
When he signed the agreement, Fort Berthold tribal chairman
George Gillette was in tears. He said, "The truth is, as everyone
knows, our Treaty of Fort Laramie . . . and our constitution are
being torn to shreds by this contract."

The Garrison Dam project was one of a number of main-stem
dams built on the Missouri River as a part of what was called
the Pick-Sloan plan. The plan was to provide flood control, irrigation, navigation, and many other potential benefits. And
frankly it has accomplished many of those goals.

But it also imposed major costs that can never be recovered on
some Indian reservations, including especially the Fort Berthold
Indian Reservation and the Standing Rock Indian Reservation.
And after the dam was constructed, there was never adequate
compensation given to the tribes for the loss they experienced.

When the project began in 1951, the population of the Fort
Berthold Indian Reservation included 356 families on 583,000

acres. Most were forced to relocate from more than 153,000 acres of flooded lands. The loss of agriculturally rich bottomlands decimated hopes of self-sufficiency for many. It affected their food supply, their health care delivery system, and much more. And for that, they received a pittance in remuneration.

I understand and have supported the larger purpose of trying to harness the Missouri River to prevent chronic flooding and provide other benefits, including irrigation and power production. But there was never a reasonable excuse to disrupt the Indian homelands, move the tribes from the bottomlands, and then fail to provide full compensation and comparable lands to the tribes so they could recover. The decision to build those dams was reasonable and necessary. But so, too, was the requirement to fully compensate the tribes with land and funding needed to replace the resource they lost.

Decades after the water project was completed, the Fort Berthold Reservation produced 20 percent of the oil from the Bakken Formation in North Dakota, creating more than $1 billion in revenue over the course of a decade, and once again, far too little of that revenue came back to help the people of the Fort Berthold Indian tribe. Most of the more than fourteen thousand members of the tribe do not benefit enough from oil royalties. Life expectancy on the reservation remains low, at fifty-seven, as compared to the rest of the state of North Dakota at seventy-nine.

There is a winding road from the past to the present, but the impact of the forced homelessness, poverty, and cultural trauma Indians experience today is obvious. The combined effect of federal ineptness and corruption within some tribes has led to predictable results.

The more predictable topics of broken families, substance abuse, gangs, poverty, and more will always be the first discussed.

But intergenerational trauma is always there, a shadow over every other discussion about Indian children.

It's probably hard for non-Indians, especially those who've been in America for more than a couple of generations, to understand what the term *intergenerational trauma* really means. But the bitter experience of life as American Indians in a country where their land was stolen and they were virtually imprisoned, massacred, starved, and tortured for a couple of centuries has left bitter memories of mistreatment that generations of Indians have inherited.

Native Americans were not even granted full U.S. citizenship until 1924.

The fight for fairness never really ended. In fact, one determined woman named Elouise Cobell, a member of the Blackfeet tribe in Montana, led a class action suit in 1996 against the Department of the Interior and the Department of the Treasury for mismanagement of Indian trust funds. Suing the U.S. government is a daunting task, but Cobell said, "If someone tells me something can't be done, I get so mad I just have to do it."

Plagued by inept or nonexistent financial records, the government's defense crumbled. She won a $3.4 billion settlement for Native Americans. She died in 2011, but her name lives on in a scholarship program generated from some of that money, called the Cobell Educational Scholarship Fund. It is designed to assist young Native American scholars. Through these scholarships, the example and strength of this unique Native American woman will live on in Indian country.

Yes, cultural trauma is real. And it continues to impose a cost on the Indian population in the United States even today.

4

There's Little Care in This Health Care System

I saw more than I can tell, and I understood more than I saw; for I was seeing in a sacred manner the shapes of things in the spirit, and the shape of all shapes as they must live together like one being.

—BLACK ELK

For American Indian children, health care is often about life and death. The tragedy is that the health care so many others in our country take for granted is not available to many Indian children. We've long known that giving children a healthy start in life is so very important, but that healthy start is simply not available to a good many Native American children.

It is certain that Tamara didn't have a healthy start. During the several days following the beating she suffered when she was two, she was abandoned in a room alone with no access to medical help. Her bones didn't heal properly as a result. But the entirety of Tamara's young life describes the failure of a health care system.

When she was sexually assaulted by a relative, there was no intervention or mental health care available to her. Her mother refused to believe it even happened. She suffered alone.

After Tamara attempted suicide in Rapid City, South Dakota,

her older sister Karla asked her to come live with her in Minneapolis.

Karla was an army veteran who served two terms in Iraq and who confirmed the details of Tamara's description of her life at home. Karla added more context to the struggles she and Tamara had as she described a bleak and often violent family life. It was a family dominated by an alcoholic mother Karla described as abusive. The children lived in fear. A passive father, also suffering from alcoholism, did nothing, she said. "What Tamara has told you about our home life is accurate," she said.

Asked if she had any pleasant memories of her home, of her mother and father, Karla pondered somberly for a moment. "No, there is nothing in my memory that recalls any pleasant times in that home."

Let that sink in. Now compare that to your own childhood.

Tamara's horrific early years wounded her inside and out. "I have nightmares and severe anxiety," she said. "The nightmares are what scare me the most. I have them two or three times a week. Sometimes in those nightmares, I will remember things from my past."

She copes as well as she can. "I just try to keep by myself. I do a lot of internalizing and try to hide a lot of what is bothering me."

That need for solitude, the need to retreat, led her to the hard streets of Minneapolis. "I lived with my sister Karla for about eight months, but Karla had others staying there as well, so I just decided to be on my own. I didn't want to bother anybody."

She had no access to health care. "I knew that I needed medical help, but it wasn't available to someone who was homeless and without any money to pay for it," Tamara said.

The Salvation Army—Help From a Stranger

The night her employer refused to drop her off under the bridge she called home, he may have saved her life. He took her to a Salvation Army shelter in Minneapolis and insisted she go inside, something Tamara, someone with an inordinate amount of pride, was loath to do. That night, he was more determined than she was. He refused to leave until she entered the shelter.

As she walked through the front door, Tamara said the place was overflowing with people, as it is on most nights. They have only twenty-five beds for women, but they are able to put twenty-five mattresses on the floor in the hallways to accommodate more women.

Tamara was shown to a mattress on the floor near the end of the hallway, and that first night was the start of nearly a year and a half that she spent at the Salvation Army. She slept on that mattress at the end of the hallway for that entire time.

Tamara recalled, "Sleeping at the Salvation Army was a challenge. There were so many men and women that they clashed. Many of them had emotional problems, and it wasn't unusual that a fight would break out at three or four in the morning, so it wasn't always easy to get rest."

Early on, she met the second person who changed her life for the better.

Kate Sherva, a social worker at the shelter, noticed Tamara almost immediately after she came to the shelter and took an interest in this young, introspective woman who carried inside a great deal of pain and confusion.

"She was quiet, seemed sad, and kept to herself," Kate said. "At our shelter, the women have to be up and out of the shelter early in the morning and are allowed back late in the afternoon,"

Kate said. "As a result, I often worked late into the night in order to have conversations with the women to learn how we can be helpful to them."

Kate was one of 1.5 million members of the Salvation Army, which was established in 1865 and globally serves some twenty-five million people annually. According to organizational statistics, the Salvation Army shelters thirty thousand Americans every night, a small percentage of the actual number of homeless citizens in the United States.

"There are some women at the shelter who don't want to go out and live on their own," Tamara said. "They would rather live in a group setting. They seem frightened of independence. The homeless shelter became their institution."

Tamara's mattress was just outside Kate's office. "One evening," Kate said, "I sat down on the mattress next to Tamara and began visiting with her. She told me about the difficulties she had with PTSD, her nightmares, and crowd anxiety. That began a discussion we had about what had happened to her and the impact it had on her life. The details of her early life seemed out of reach for Tamara. She just had hazy memories of bad things happening to her early in her life that were causing her continuing problems."

The Salvation Army provided a balance of normalcy and stability to a young woman who had known little, but her mind and heart had been profoundly scarred. No sustainable treatment was available. It's a situation that affects many Americans.

Our response to mental health issues across the country is clearly lagging. It's everybody's issue, and it's critical in chronically stressed and underserved segments of the population.

But there are beacons of hope. Kate Sherva made a difference for Tamara.

"I knew that there was very little mental health help available for Tamara," she said, "but I thought I might be able to find another way to help her. I told her I would like to search for some options that might allow her to move out of the shelter and find a place to live. I began working to help her meet the eligibility requirements for a disability assistance program that was available in Minnesota. I also worked to get her some vouchers for food assistance and also to put her on a list for low-income housing. Then I was able to connect her to some medical help to get something for her PTSD and headaches. Eventually, the assistance payments began, the housing assistance followed, and Tamara was able to find a place to live and to have some meager funding on which to live.

"Over the period she spent at the shelter, we became better acquainted, and Tamara began to open up to me a bit. I could feel we were bonding, and she trusted me. During the year and a half that Tamara was at our shelter, we became friends, and I was determined to help her get on her feet. I saw this quiet, shy young woman writing poetry and doing drawings, and we had long talks about her health and her life. She is smart and curious, and I was so anxious to help her and give her an opportunity to straighten out her life."

Each day, the women had to leave the shelter. Many of them, including Tamara, went to the library. Tamara said she signed up for some classes. She read books and used the computer, which led to our reconnecting—and to this book. It created an opportunity to bring to light the desperate condition in which many indigenous people find themselves with the hope that when people understand the gravity of the problem, they will be moved to do something about it.

Although statistics are vital to understanding such issues, it's the human condition, the personal stories of anguish and survival, that can move people to action.

Most of the delivery of health care for Native Americans comes from the Indian Health Service (IHS). It manages clinics and some hospitals on Indian reservations throughout the nation.

There are two problems with the IHS. First, it is estimated that the funding made available for the IHS is only enough to serve about 50 percent of the needs among the Indian population. That means there is full-scale health care rationing on many reservations. In normal circumstances, that would be a national scandal.

The second problem is that the IHS is riddled with incompetence. Yes, there are some wonderful people who work there, but the reality is there are too many stories of incompetence and second-rate medicine being practiced.

It's hard to fully describe the dysfunction at the IHS. New directors come and go, and yet the system seems impervious to change or improvement. Corruption is a problem. Investigations have revealed it to be an agency where relatives hire relatives. Incompetence is ignored, and bad employees are often transferred to the next service unit. Some criminal activity, such as stealing drugs from hospitals, is excused or minimized. Some members of the medical staff were found not to be properly credentialed even though they were treating patients. Sexual harassment was tolerated without any meaningful punishment.

Over the past couple of years, Dan Frosch, along with Christopher Weaver and a team of investigative reporters at *The Wall Street Journal,* exposed the story of Patrick Weber, who was accused of sexually abusing young boys over many decades while serving as an IHS doctor on Indian reservations. Complaints by parents and children about the abuse during that time fell on deaf ears at the IHS. The reporting by the *Journal* disclosed that rather than conducting a serious investigation of the sexual abuse alleged by the children and their parents, IHS simply transferred the doctor to another IHS facility, putting more children at risk of abuse.

Weber was finally convicted of child sexual abuse and is now serving an eighteen-year prison sentence in South Dakota. He is appealing the conviction. But it's clear that investigative reporters for *The Wall Street Journal* did what the IHS was unwilling to do in this case: protect Native American children. It is another shameful example of how some young Native Americans have been victimized by the IHS.

This dysfunction in the Indian Health Service is not just a matter of inconvenience—it is too often punishing Native American children.

A Princess Lost

Ta'Shon Rain Little Light was a beautiful, bright-eyed Crow Indian girl full of energy. Her aunt described her as a happy girl who was always smiling and, even at age five, was excited to put on her traditional Indian dance dress and participate in the tribal dances. The day she died, Ta'Shon Rain Little Light was at a hotel in Disney World on a trip sponsored by the Make-A-Wish Foundation for terminally ill patients. Her dying wish was to see the Cinderella Castle. Even that was denied.

I learned about Ta'Shon at a U.S. Senate hearing I was holding with Montana senator John Tester on the Crow Agency Indian reservation in Montana on the subject of the Indian health care system. The room was full of concerned Native Americans. They knew firsthand the fatal shortcomings of health care on the reservation. In the audience was Ta'Shon's aunt Ada, who was determined to make sure we senators knew, too, by telling us about the egregious mistakes that resulted in the suffering and death of her niece.

When the hearing began, Ada didn't wait for others to talk. She rose from her seat in the audience and began walking down the aisle to the front where the senators sat. In both hands over her head she raised a very large poster board with a blown-up color photograph of a beautiful young child.

"This is a photograph of my niece Ta'Shon Rain Little Light," she said with a strong and clear voice loud enough to be heard across the room.

"I want you to take a long look at the picture of this beautiful young girl and listen to her story," she implored the senators as she continued to approach the stage.

"My niece Ta'Shon Rain Little Light died a horrible, painful death at age five because she did not get the basic health care that was promised to Native American citizens."

By then, Aunt Ada had the full attention of the senators, and you could hear a pin drop in the hearing room as she told the sad story about the girl in the photograph.

"This is Ta'Shon," she said, "and she was the happiest little girl you ever saw."

Through her tears, Ada described a young child who was normally very active, but who, over a week's time, had lost her appetite, stopped eating and moving around, and complained to her mother that her stomach hurt. Her mother became very concerned and took Ta'Shon to the IHS on the reservation.

Her mother said the doctor examined Ta'Shon and diagnosed her problem as "depression." The doctor prescribed some medicine for depression and sent her home.

Admittedly, there is a lot of depression on Indian reservations, but for a cheery five-year-old? It didn't make any sense to her mother. Even if the diagnosis had been correct, IHS is mostly limited to basic psychiatric emergency care due to budget constraints and personnel problems, so Ta'Shon wouldn't have received much help for the doctor's diagnosis.

In the weeks that followed, Ta'Shon's pain grew more intense, and her condition worsened. Her family took her back to the Indian health clinic several more times, but the doctor at the clinic insisted that the young girl was depressed and continued prescribing additional medicine for depression. Finally, after intense prodding from the family, the doctors at the clinic did a series of blood tests, which they had previously not done. They found nothing in the tests that alarmed them, so they continued diagnosing her condition as depression.

Ta'Shon's condition grew worse and she suffered a collapsed lung. Finally she was taken to an emergency room at the nearest hospital in Billings, Montana, off the Crow reservation. There, doctors quickly saw the gravity of her condition and immediately airlifted her to the Children's Hospital Colorado in Denver.

On the day she arrived at Children's Hospital Colorado, they conducted a series of sophisticated tests and images, and they found the cause of Ta'Shon's illness. It was the worst news possible. The doctors asked the family to come to the hospital conference room. It was there they gave the family the devastating news. It was cancer! Terminal cancer! A rare cancer that was not treatable! The kind of news that can drop a parent to their knees. They were told Ta'Shon had only a few months to live.

Days later, heartbroken by the news, Ta'Shon and her family traveled back to the mobile home they lived in on the reservation. They put a hospital bed in their small living room so that Ta'Shon would be comfortable and constantly with her family.

This is cancer's begrudging gift: to allow loved ones a long good-bye.

Then, the clouds parted just for a moment. Ta'Shon, although very ill and becoming weaker by the day, was thrilled when her family was contacted by the Make-A-Wish Foundation and asked if Ta'Shon had a special wish. Ta'Shon told her parents that she wanted to go to Cinderella Castle. She had always dreamed of seeing it.

Ta'Shon's wish almost came true.

The evening they arrived at the Disney World hotel in Orlando, Ta'Shon was very weak. Her mother rocked her in her arms, sensing Ta'Shon's time was short. "Mommy, I'm so sorry to be sick," she said. Words that would break the heart of any parent. The next morning, just before leaving the hotel to visit the Cinderella Castle, Ta'Shon Rain Little Light took her last breath.

A week later, at the funeral held for Ta'Shon, all of her little friends arrived dressed as Cinderella—a poignant, poetic good-bye to a young child who never had a chance.

Aunt Ada could not have known the impact her walk down the aisle of that auditorium would have at that Senate hearing. As she carried that large photograph of that precious child above her head and told her story, the room went silent. Tears formed in some eyes. Throats grew thick. It was an unforgettable moment for those who witnessed it.

Later, with Ada's consent, I took that large poster board photo of Ta'Shon to the floor of the U.S. Senate every day during debate on the Indian Health Care Improvement Act, legislation that had been stalled for seventeen years.

I placed that large photograph poster of a beautiful five-year-old girl with bright eyes, wearing a colorful traditional dance dress, on a chart stand next to my Senate desk.

I wanted every senator to have to look deep into those soulful eyes and the face of that beautiful child and see the life and death of a five-year-old girl who suffered and died because of second-class health care. I told her story again and again to the U.S. senators. I wanted them to remember Ta'Shon Rain Little Light, whose life was cut short at age five.

When you put a face to statistics, our humanity emerges. At long last, seventeen years too late, Congress did act to reauthorize the Indian Health Care Improvement Act. It was a step forward, but it could not fix the myriad of problems facing the Indian Health Service.

The epilogue to the story about Ta'Shon came from her mother when she received the news that the health care bill the Senate passed was dedicated to Ta'Shon. During the bittersweet conversation, she wistfully remembered that one day when Ta'Shon was sick, Ta'Shon and her dad watched a movie about Ray Charles on television together when Ta'Shon asked, "Is Ray Charles dead, and if he is, how can he still be famous?"

Her dad replied, "Yes, he died, but some people are still famous after they die."

Ta'Shon replied, "Well, Dad, then maybe I'll be famous someday!"

Maybe so, Ta'Shon! Maybe so!

Ta'Shon Rain Little Light was just another victim of a seemingly mindless bureaucracy that has good people within who are trapped in a ponderous, underfunded maze. But experiences like hers happen day after day, human after suffering human, a powerful reminder of our failure to provide the kind of health care we have promised to Native Americans.

Maybe, had they discovered her tumor earlier, Ta'Shon would have survived. No one knows for certain. But we do know that the health care provided at the IHS facility fell far short. She never had a chance.

Don't Get Sick After June

There's a great debate raging across America today about health care. There are those who see it as a basic right of citizenship, an obligation of society to help those suffering. Others take more of a law-of-the-jungle attitude; they see the inability to afford care almost as a personal failing. You just have to work harder. Bootstraps, people!

Traditionally, though, most Americans have held sacred our Constitution and its requirement that we abide by treaties. And it is the treaties that have made solemn promises to provide health care to Native Americans. We do such a terrible job of keeping that promise.

There's a reason they say on many reservations, "Don't get sick after June."

At the Indian health care facilities on reservations, there is a program called Contract Health Service, which provides the opportunity for tribal members to be sent to a larger medical facility for their treatment if the procedure can't be done locally and it is considered a potential loss of life or limb. That program exists because the existing IHS hospitals seldom have the capability of treating the more serious health issues that can threaten the lives of patients; those patients must be sent to other hospitals who have the expertise to treat those problems.

However, the Contract Health fund is also far short of the amount of money needed to treat those patients. It means that the money for Contract Health runs out quickly, and when it does, those who are very sick will likely be denied the funding.

In one memorable case that was described to the Senate Indian Affairs Committee, a woman named Adele Hale Baker went to the health center on the Three Affiliated Tribes Reservation in North Dakota with what was thought to be a heart attack. She was put in an ambulance to be transferred to a hospital in a city eighty miles away where they would be better equipped to deal with the health emergency, presumably for treatment to be paid for with Contract Health funds.

However, when she arrived at the hospital, the hospital attendants who were removing her from the ambulance noticed a handwritten sheet of paper someone had taped to her thigh, appallingly informing the hospital that if they admitted this patient, they would be responsible for the costs because the Contract Health fund for the tribe had run out. How sick does one have to be to expect the kind of medical treatment so many other Americans take for granted?

Other testimony of outrageous health care delivered to Native Americans before the Senate Committee on Indian Affairs described a woman who had nearly unbearable pain in her knee because of the loss of cartilage resulting in bone rubbing on bone. She was told by the IHS doctor to wrap her knee in cabbage leaves and rest it. Unbelievable! That story was told to the committee by a doctor who finally saw the patient and began responsible treatment.

Given the state of health care delivery to Native Americans, it isn't surprising that in some areas Native Americans have a much shorter life span than other Americans. "We've lost faith in the IHS, but we have no alternatives to go anywhere else," Lisa White Pipe, a tribal council member for the Rosebud Sioux, told *The Wall Street Journal* after her father died due to a delay in cancer treatment that she blames on the agency.

The issues of underfunding and incompetent management at the Indian Health Service can be cured, but this failed bureaucracy won't be healed without restructuring, and when one considers the ineffective bloat that plagues America's health care system, it is obvious we have a long way to go. As we do some national soul-searching about health care, we must ask ourselves if for-profit health care is ethical. Should the size of one's wallet be the measure of your right to life?

"People are dying here as a result of the care they are not receiving, or the care they are receiving," said U.S. senator John Barrasso (R-WY), a former chair of the Indian Affairs Committee. "As both a doctor and a senator, I find the level of dysfunction completely unacceptable. Not only does the United States government have a trust responsibility they must fulfill, but failures of the Indian Health Service should never result in the loss of life."

Those words were sincere, but can they translate into positive change? Time will tell. History echoes similar pronouncements. As early as 1926, the U.S. government studied Native American health, and a 1928 report said that the health status of Native Americans was intolerable. And here we are . . .

The U.S. Commission on Civil Rights issued a report entitled *Broken Promises* in 2004. Their prescription for the system "involves a holistic approach, including considerations of education, housing, and economic opportunity, as well as empowerment through self-determination and self-governance."

The disparity of treatment between Native Americans and other Americans truly is a civil rights issue. The report said, "Racial and ethnic bias and discrimination, cause and contribute to Native American health disparities. Conscious discrimination is not as common as the unconscious bias frequently displayed by health care providers serving Native American communities . . .

Studies have discovered that, while unintentional, health care providers make treatment decisions based on their cultural and racial biases and stereotypes."

The Desperate Need for Mental Health Care

One of the most serious deficiencies of the Indian Health Service is the lack of mental health treatment that is so desperately needed among the Indian population.

When it comes to mental health care, an overwhelming number of American citizens are underserved, with tragic results. It's worse in rural areas. In western parts of the country, veteran suicides are much higher than in other locales, in part because of the distance between patients and Veterans Affairs hospitals.

Veterans suffering from PTSD were committing suicide at a horrifying rate—twenty-one a day in 2013. In states like New Mexico, Montana, Nevada, and Utah, the suicide rate for veterans is much higher than the national rate. I'm certain it is because so little mental health treatment is available in large, sparsely populated states.

Native Americans are a population that suffers at a higher risk for mental health disorders than other racial and ethnic groups, and that is attributed to the high rates of homelessness, incarceration, alcohol and drug abuse, and stress and trauma of reservation life. And it's also the case that many Indian reservations are far from population centers and very little mental health treatment is available on the reservations.

Only recently have Americans become more aware of this issue, but it's been happening for a long time. Despair sets in early. From 1985 to 1996, indigenous children committed suicide at two and one-half times the rate of white children.

Teen suicide, along with so many other challenges faced by Indian children, points directly to the absence of opportunities Indian children have to access health care. Again, they're near the front lines of an epidemic of suicide in this country that points to a deeper cultural sickness. Seemingly, for the most disenfranchised among us, things are getting worse instead of better.

In discussions about health care in America, mental health care is often missing, but the serious lack of good mental health care can trigger a cascade of other health issues. The Department of Housing and Urban Development (HUD) reports that, like Tamara, an estimated 26 percent of homeless adults staying in shelters have some mental illness, while an estimated 46 percent have severe mental illness and/or substance-use disorders, all factors that impact physical well-being—issues like heart disease, asthma, weakened immune system, obesity, and gastrointestinal issues. Depression can lead to chronic fatigue, insomnia, and sensitivity to aches and pains due to dysfunction of neurotransmitters in the brain.

The rate of depression in youths increased from 5.9 percent to 8.2 percent from 2012 to 2015, and 56 percent of adults with mental illness go untreated because it's internal, less evident, and we are slow to connect the dots between mental anguish and resultant physical symptoms.

Can you imagine any other debilitating disease going untreated at an increased rate of 56 percent? When we stop preening about the excellence of American health care—and many aspects of it are excellent—we must admit we have fallen woefully short, and none have been shortchanged as much as Native Americans. And while the philosophical arguments go on about whether a modest baseline of health care ought to be provided to all Americans, the fact remains that this country has made a solemn promise to Native Americans to do just that, and we've failed miserably.

These are life-and-death issues as indicated by the epidemic of suicides among Native American children and across the nation.

As illustrated with Tamara's story, there's an interconnectedness between the lack of mental health care and grave spiritual, societal, and fiscal costs. As we examine the specific issues facing Native Americans, it's important to see them in context. In every case, issues that plague Native Americans affect the broader population—yes, usually to a lesser degree—but they truly do serve as a canary in the coal mine to alert us to systemic problems. At some level, we're all affected. We all pay a price when segments of our population suffer. As Black Elk said, "[We] must live together like one being."

One of the predictable results of untreated mental illness is incarceration.

Native Americans are incarcerated at a very high rate. *The Wall Street Journal* reported in 2015 that Native Americans are jailed at a 38 percent higher rate than the national average. Indian men are jailed at four times the rate of white men and Indian women at six times the rate of other women, and Native American youths are 30 percent more likely to be referred to juvenile court than have charges dropped. Those figures ought to set off alarms; they are combined indications of a community plagued by dysfunction and a biased judicial system. If incarceration is a measurement of the health of a society, America is running a high fever, and Native Americans, especially, are burning up.

While the United States has only 5 percent of the world's population, it has nearly 25 percent of its prisoners—about 2.2 million people. The sheer number of mentally ill Americans behind bars is a symptom of an unwell society. I should persuade all Americans to press for more and better diagnosis and treatment for those who suffer from mental illness.

Yes, America is a great country, but we need to take our blinders off and admit there are problems that will impede our progress as a nation unless we address them. Only then can we continue to evolve and truly live up to our ideals.

Astonishingly, *The Journal of Pediatrics* reported that 41 percent of young American adults have been arrested by the time they are twenty-three. The Department of Justice reports that 6.6 percent of all people will do time in prison. More than half are diagnosed with a mental disorder. Not surprisingly, the dangers and solitude of prison life exacerbate and create even more mental health issues.

According to a report by the National Research Council, one out of every one hundred adults in America is behind bars, a rate five to ten times higher than in Western Europe or other democracies. There's an incredible societal and financial cost to prison—about $60 billion annually on state and federal prisons, according to the Pew Research Center.

The fiscal consequences of this issue are critical, because compassion doesn't move everyone. Some are moved more by the monetary aspects of an issue. And it does have to make sense. For example, when it comes to treating drug addicts, based on a study from the Justice Policy Institute in 2004, the cost of treatment in Maryland was a fifth of the cost of prison.

When as a nation will we understand that being proactive in all aspects is more effective and less expensive than being reactive? Frustratingly, the programs or solutions proposed are often branded as handouts when, in fact, they make sound financial sense in the most conservative sense of the word *investment*. There's a difference between a handout and an investment.

Investments in education pay off, although we don't invest enough. Investment in the health of our fellow Americans speaks to our sense of decency as well as basic common sense. And frankly, sometimes a handout is necessary if we pretend to have any sense of morality. The existing system on reservations, in VA hospitals, and in for-profit health care is cumbersome, ineffective in many aspects, and wasteful.

Truly having an honest, bipartisan, national conversation about these issues with a willingness to compromise is necessary. The exclusion of Americans from health care is immoral and repugnant. Unfortunately, if we hold to form, we will wait until the system implodes, and then in a reactive manner, we will do a patchwork "fix" and kick the can down the road. The implosion may have already begun.

Dialogue and leadership can and ultimately will make the difference. In the absence of leadership, let there be dialogue. Amid the din of voices, can we begin to clarify our national priorities? Most great societal change comes from the people and not from the government. The power of the republic is in the hands of the American people.

At the close of the Constitutional Convention of 1787, Benjamin Franklin was asked by a woman as he left Independence Hall, "Well, Doctor, what have we got—a republic or a monarchy?"

Franklin replied, "A republic, if you can keep it."

If.

One of the more promising developments in health care is that more physicians than ever before understand the impact of mental stresses on physical health. The connection between mind and spirit and body.

While MDs practice allopathic medicine, the classical form of medicine focused on the diagnosis and treatment of human diseases, DOs employ osteopathic medicine, which takes a more holistic approach. The patient is viewed as a whole person rather than treating the symptoms alone. A DO also places emphasis on the prevention of disease. Of the eight hundred thousand physicians in the country, about fifty thousand are DOs.

That approach is closer to the general Native American concept of health, which revolves around the concept that man is part of nature and that health is a matter of balance and harmony with all things of the universe. Native Americans have a saying, "We are all related," and the concept is that all things exist in relationship to one another; it's about living in harmony with the earth and the environment.

The environment on Indian reservations has resulted in daunting health care challenges, especially for children. The incidence of diabetes is epidemic. On some reservations, it is up to ten and twelve times the rate for other Americans.

And violence is also a contributor to the health care deficiency.

The amount of violence resulting in physical harm on the reservations is devastating. Native Americans are victims of violent crime at double the rate of other Americans—88 percent of the violent crime committed against Indian women is by non-Natives. The prevalence of substance abuse, the tragedy of teen suicide, the dramatic rise in obesity, the list goes on . . .

To understand the shortage of funding for Indian health care, consider this: Per-person spending on health care for Native Americans is about $3,500 per year, about half of what is spent on inmates in federal prisons. And as underserved as military veterans have historically been, the government spends about three times as much per person for them.

That disparity describes the failure of presidents and Congress to properly fund the health care needs Native Americans were promised. It's obvious that Indian health care is just not a priority for the U.S. government despite the responsibility and the grand promises that have been made over many decades.

That doesn't mean the Native American community is stagnantly sitting on its hands. Where there are issues, there are Indian leaders working to make a difference.

Back to the Roots of Healthy Eating

When it comes to healthier living, the work of a young Native American woman from the Blackfeet tribe in Montana is especially impressive. Her name is Mariah Gladstone, and she has begun an inspiring journey to restore the health of Native Americans through good nutrition and healthy food. She describes a time past when meat from the bison and elk that roamed the prairies as well as the grains, vegetables, and berries that were once plentiful on Indian lands were the foundation of healthy, balanced Native American diets.

In a compelling TEDx Talk video on YouTube, Mariah describes the gravity facing today's Native people from obesity, diabetes, heart disease, and more of which are linked to diet. She also describes approaches to good nutrition and traditional food preparation that can begin to restore the health of Native Americans. It's a lesson all of us would do well to take to heart.

Mariah is a graduate from Columbia University studying environmental engineering. But her passion led her to create a YouTube channel to create something called Indigikitchen, teaching American Indians about the culture and history of eating natural foods and how to prepare them.

She's one of those young Native Americans who is not waiting for change, who is forcing positive change in innovative ways using new technology to instruct Native Americans in traditional, healthier ways. Her work offers real change and provides better health to give hope and strength to the First Americans.

Mariah describes the history of Native American tribes that have spent centuries on the land with plentiful food from meat, root vegetables, and berries that were a major part of the Native American healthy diet.

When the Indian population was forced from their native lands and relocated to reservations where there was little opportunity to hunt or raise crops, their diet changed in a dramatic and unhealthy way. The bison herds had been destroyed, and the new, unproductive land on the reservations was not capable of providing the healthy foods the Indian populations were accustomed to eating. In large part, that resulted in the epidemic of obesity, diabetes, heart disease, and other diseases in recent generations.

Mariah has created Indigikitchen to instruct and mentor Native American populations about the selection and preparation of foods that have existed for Native Americans for many centuries.

Mariah and other young Native Americans are working to teach Indian tribes about nutrition and health education. But, even when a body gets the right nutrition, there are still inevitable medical issues. And Native Americans across the country are still reliant on the Indian Health Service (IHS).

Investigations by Congress and by the Government Accountability Office (GAO) have severely criticized how the delivery of health care has been handled or mishandled. All of this is occurring while major health risks are growing rapidly among the Indian population.

Obesity and Diabetes

For example, the rate of obesity has become epidemic among Indian tribes, including with their youth. The effects of cheap, prepackaged foods with labels listing ingredients that sound like a science project affect all Americans, but since they are cheaper than fresh, wholesome foods, those struggling with poverty eat more of them. Poverty runs deeper on reservations, and it is evident when it comes to Indian health.

Studies show that nearly 44 percent of Native Americans eighteen years of age and over are obese compared to 29 percent of other Americans. In addition, obesity is a serious problem among Native American children. One in four children between the ages of two and five is obese, and one in three children between the ages of six and eighteen is obese.

The dramatic increase in obesity among Native Americans is something that has happened in just a few generations, and most researchers believe it relates to low-income families eating less expensive foods much higher in fat content—and a less active lifestyle than previous generations.

Closely related to the obesity epidemic is the deadly increase in diabetes. For all American Indian and Alaska Native adults, the number of diagnosed cases of diabetes compared to other Americans is more than double.

But for the Native American youth aged ten to nineteen, the rate of diagnosed diabetes is nine times higher than for other American youth. The disease seems to be spiraling out of control. The increase in diagnosed diabetes among young Native Americans is up 110 percent.

This is just sterile data, but anyone who lives with diabetes understands that it isn't about statistics. It is about the chronic and relentless difficulty managing that disease twenty-four hours a day. Diabetics living on Indian reservations and in rural areas of America in general have great difficulty getting access to the treatment and monitoring they desperately need.

The complications of diabetes-related illnesses are double the rate of the rest of the population. The prevalence of heart disease and stroke are two to four times higher as a result of having diabetes. And finally, people with diagnosed diabetes have double the health care expenditure than persons without diabetes.

As a result of the dramatic increase in kidney failure resulting from diabetes, the Native American population struggles to have enough dialysis centers to treat them. Some tribes now have dialysis centers on the reservation while others transport their patients many miles twice a week to be hooked up to the dialysis machine. It is sobering to understand that patients are so lacking in adequate treatment for diabetes that it sometimes even results in amputations.

The IHS estimates that their annual congressional appropriations have only met about half of American Indian and Alaska Natives' health care needs, but because the health care rationing that results from that is happening on Indian reservations, it is out of sight and out of mind for most Americans. The IHS is a big, ungainly organization rife with the thick glue of bureaucracy. Incapable of doing even some of the most routine things, it often provides second-class health care to a group of American citizens who need it most.

And what about the state of health care nationally? Entrenched corporate interests and government bureaucracies are not easily budged. Health care comprises nearly a fifth of the national economy. It's unsustainable and unequal, and that, in large part, is why people are dying.

The Affordable Care Act had the right intentions, subsidized the cost of health care for the most vulnerable, and offered a key provision—even those with preexisting conditions could get care. It was a partial, incomplete solution lacking a public option—Medicare for All—that would have allowed a transition to a more sustainable health care system. However, for those in the middle and businesses that didn't qualify for subsidies, the cost of premiums continued to grow just as it had for decades, often in double-digit percentage increases. The backlash opened the door to the removal of the mandated purchase of insurance, which meant fewer Americans would be insured and those that were would pay even more. The intent of some hard-core conservatives is as it has always been: to eliminate social safety nets, to roll back the gains of the middle class under FDR and LBJ. Fortunately most Americans understand the value and importance of these programs.

Astonishingly, in 2018, the Trump administration, exhibiting remarkable cluelessness about the responsibilities and realities of reservation health care, asserted that before receiving Medicaid benefits in some states, tribal members must first have a job.

First of all, that completely ignores the federal government's promises of health care under treaty, and secondly, it ignorantly supposes that people wouldn't work if they had the means to get to a job and if jobs were readily available. Most people in most places want to work and better themselves.

Trump's Health and Human Services administrator, Seema Verma, said, "Doctors know that helping individuals rise out of poverty can be the best medicine!" She's not wrong, but the mandate is wrongheaded.

Mary Smith, a Cherokee and former head of IHS during the

Obama administration, said viewing this as some kind of handout is fiction. "They've paid through land and massacres," she said.

As astoundingly misguided and vapid as this approach is, it has created conversation, and that may well shine a light on the complex issues facing those in poverty, not just on the reservations but across America.

If we truly focus on the issue of health care on reservations with a fresh vision, successful change there may well inspire the same through our national health care system.

It comes down to *awareness*.

Then, *will*.

And finally, *leadership*.

5

Teach the Children Well

Education is the most powerful weapon which you can use to change the world.

—NELSON MANDELA

For Tamara, school was hard.

She had a lot working against her, but Tamara made it through grade school and actually thrived at a boarding school in Pierre, South Dakota, through eighth grade, but she was not able to get through high school because of family instability.

Home itself was a transitory thing. She said her parents often fought, so Tamara was bounced between two high schools in Mobridge and Wakpala, South Dakota, seventeen miles apart, each time her mother moved, which was often, leaving Tamara uprooted and hopelessly behind in her studies as she was jolted from one school to the other. "I couldn't keep up on my schoolwork," she said.

Meanwhile, at home, Tamara was either mistreated or neglected.

When she was fifteen, she ran away for the first time.

"When I returned, I would end up in my grandma's care," she remembered. Even there, she wasn't safe. She continued to be sexually assaulted by a member of the extended family. "I ran away from there, too, and I was caught. Then I was sent to a foster home as a ward of the state, but that ended when I got in trouble there for having a man in my room. So I was sent to a group home."

The man became her boyfriend and the father of her oldest child, Brenden, born in 2010, who lives with his father and family at the Cheyenne River Indian Reservation in South Dakota. Tamara has described his home as very loving and stable.

She has another child, Aidan, three years younger than Brenden, from another relationship. Aidan lives with a foster mother in the Pacific Northwest.

Tamara is overwhelmed by psychological issues, and her inability to be a mother to her two children haunts her.

"I feel like I'm a bad person," she said. "But I know I'm not capable of being a mother right now. I think most people would look down on me for not being able to take care of my children, but I know that I just don't have the capability with my PTSD and other issues to take care of them. I wish with all my heart that things were different."

Tamara fled from the group home, too. She and another girl eluded authorities for a month or so before Tamara, with nowhere to go, turned herself in and was sent to a facility in Aberdeen, South Dakota, that focused on addiction treatment, "despite the fact that at that point I had never touched any drugs and I didn't even smoke," she said. (Tamara says she doesn't drink but admits to smoking pot on occasion as a way of coping with PTSD.)

Sadly, Tamara is just one representative of a cycle of hopelessness that permeates too much of life on the reservation. Poverty often leads to despair, depression, and substance abuse; that leads to instability in the home and, often, all manner of child abuse, and so the lifeline of education remains out of reach for many children, who are simply in survival mode.

While a stable, loving family environment is no guarantee of educational achievement, that kind of base gives a child a much better chance. Education is the second pillar that can, and often does, play a major role in the life of Native American children. It's the great leveler in America; aside from being born into wealth or winning the lottery, education is the single most transformative tool in a democracy. All people are created equal, but not all have equal opportunities.

Indian children, some forty-eight thousand in 183 reservation schools, graduate at the lowest rate of any demographic—at a 67 percent rate in 2015 as compared to 80 percent nationally. In North Dakota, for example, the overall graduation rate was nearly 90 percent but just 65 percent on reservations.

The struggles confronting education on the reservations are significant. When I toured the school in Cannon Ball, North Dakota, during one of my reservation visits, I found a crowded classroom with desks an inch apart in a building in which a portion had been condemned. Rosie Two Bears, a fourth grader, looked up at me and asked, "Mr. Senator, are you going to build us a new school?" A heartbreaking plea. Another young girl on the reservation, when asked by her teacher what she wanted for Christmas, said she hoped to have the electricity turned on at home so she could study at night.

It's not too difficult to describe the shortcomings of Indian education, but it would be a mistake to believe there aren't also some wonderful stories of accomplishment. For example, a sixteen-year-old boy in California had an audacious study plan for his classmates that became a model for success.

Dahkota Kicking Bear Brown Had an Idea—NERDS

Dahkota Kicking Bear Brown reminds us that doing the right thing can have a profound and lasting effect in education.

Dahkota is a member of the Wilton Band of Miwok Indians in California. As an eighth grader at a Native American school near the reservation in California, Dahkota Brown saw that many of his friends in school were just as capable as he was, but they weren't studying and were, in some cases, just too proud to admit they were impossibly behind in their studies and could no longer keep up. In other cases, they lacked motivation and pride in their schoolwork.

A friend of Dahkota's who played with him on the football team was failing in school and about to be kicked off the team. Dahkota decided to try something unusual. He went to his friend on the football team and told him that he would stay after school with him for an hour every day to help him catch up and keep up with his studies. His friend was appreciative and accepted Dahkota's help.

The two of them decided to invite others to join them after school, and the study group named themselves the NERDS Club—*Native Education Raising Dedicated Students.* A clever name. The purpose of the club was to get kids to work together on their studies and help each other become students who would succeed at their classwork.

Dahkota had managed to convince football players of the importance of their educations, to be part of a club that self-identifies as NERDS. Because it was a club started by a couple of young athletes, it was seen as a trendy approach to working together to study and improve. Amazingly, it began to work. It became cool for Dahkota and his teammates to be in

NERDS. That acceptance drew other students to the new club.

While some resisted becoming dedicated students, most found it an opportunity to catch up on their studies and be part of a successful new way to pull their failing grades up and to begin receiving passing grades. In a short time, those who had previously been in danger of failing in their classes and becoming ineligible to participate on athletic teams were getting passing grades. Those who were getting Ds and Fs were now getting Bs and Cs.

The boy who was the best player on the football team was a special interest of Dahkota's.

"He was one of the most athletic kids on the team, and I knew that not being able to play football is what threatened him the most," Dahkota said. "So, I wanted to help him to continue his education and also to play on the team. I invited him to work together with me after school for the rest of the year, and I helped him make up missed assignments and stay on top of current work. At the end of the school year, he was earning As and Bs on his report card. He continued that progress and graduated from high school four years later with a 3.8 GPA while starring at running back.

"More than that, he was the one who really got NERDS rolling. He spread the word to other Native students about how much help working after school had been for him. Before I knew it, he had a whole group of us working together. NERDS has been growing ever since."

What Dahkota inspired flowered like blossoms in the sun. "One of the students who joined early was a seventh grader," Dahkota recounted. "When Elyssia joined, she was not able to maintain a C average in her studies, so she was put in a class for slow learners. When she joined NERDS, everything changed.

She created the logo for the club and was very active throughout high school. Soon she was earning straight As. She was invited to the White House Tribal Youth gathering and met the First Lady [Michelle Obama]. But her major achievement was graduating from high school with a 4.0 GPA, and she is now off to a prestigious academy pursuing her dreams of becoming a special effects artist. All of this from someone designated as a 'slow learner.'"

Dahkota, at the age of seventeen, became the youngest White House education advisor in history and met with President Obama many times over the course of Obama's presidency.

What a lesson, what a template Dahkota Brown provided. It wasn't the pressure of parents or the threats from teachers that caused a change in the fortunes of these kids; it was an enterprising young student who knew his friends' potential and found a clever and ingenious way to have students work together to help one another. Making academic success a part of athletic participation was one result, but allowing kids to believe in their own ability was the most important part.

Dahkota's tribe and school both recognized that a sixteen-year-old kid had created something remarkable. His school and family were proud and supportive, and he was recognized by the Center for Native American Youth as a Champion for Change. At age seventeen, Dahkota took his NERDS program to three other schools in his region with the same results. And while the NERDS program is still working to help students, Dahkota Brown is now at Stanford University. But I know we will hear more from this talented young Native American.

It's important to recognize the challenges and dysfunction in Indian education, but it is also important to describe the inspirational successes, many by some outstanding young kids who are making a difference every day. There are so many things that are critical for Indian children to thrive, starting with good parenting, and education is not far behind; the ability to get a first-rate education is a stepping-stone to opportunity.

The connection between the extreme poverty on most reservations and the shortcomings of the educational system is not hard to make. On one hand, poverty contributes to the instability of the family, but communal poverty means the tax base isn't there to fund infrastructure.

Children whose lives are stressed by poverty typically suffer from poor nutrition and a higher incidence of health problems. Incessant hunger among Native American children makes it hard to study. Typically, children living in poverty aren't exposed to a rich vocabulary or thoughtful conversations about the world around them. The family is in survival mode.

Even in a place of such extreme poverty, Tamara felt poorer than many of her peers. She recalled, "The first time I ever bought any clothes from a store was when I was sixteen or so. I was a ward of the state, and the foster care mother in whose care I was placed took me to a store because she was given an allowance for clothes for me.

"In grade school, I knew the other kids had more than I had. I never really thought about being poor, because all I had was what I had. But I was always aware that others had backpacks, rulers, pencils, and other things that I didn't have. I saw the other kids in school who had cool stuff that I knew I would never get. The only things we ever got for school were from the dollar store."

Stressful environments, of which Tamara's was an extreme but sadly not isolated example, manifest in the classroom. Some children who have a difficult home life may act out aggressively in school. Others, like Tamara, disconnect and take a passive route. They go silent. They endure, but they don't learn as well as others.

A Teacher's Story

Harriet Howe, who taught science on three different reservation schools in the Dakotas in a career that covered three decades, compared the experience of teaching on the reservation to teaching in a rural white school. "The reservation was mentally exhausting in a way I hadn't experienced before."

She said the uncertainty and abuse suffered in many home environments left her with students who were sleep-deprived. In many cases, she suspected mental and physical abuse, some of which manifested itself in depression and illness. "They always had colds," she said. Drug and alcohol abuse is prevalent. She'd heard stories of fourth graders experimenting with pot. At pre-school screenings, "maybe a third of them seemed to suffer from fetal alcohol syndrome."

When she confided to a colleague that she thought a student suffered from depression, he said, "It's the reservation. Everyone's depressed!"

Still, with a balance of compassion, discipline, and perseverance, Howe was able to reach many students who began to share their feelings.

One troubled student gave her a poem that included the lines:

> *I'm numb to the pain, numb to the blood*
> *Too numb to realize what's happening*

"There's such a sense of utter despair and hopelessness," Howe said. In her last eight years teaching at McLaughlin, South Dakota, and Fort Yates, North Dakota, she lost thirteen students to suicide. "I had them in class, loved them, hugged them, tried to counsel them, and lost them. There's only so much you can do. There's only eight hours in which they feel safe."

Another student reached out to Howe in a letter that read:

> *This is what I want you to know so I don't flunk. I am finding it hard to care about anything. I just lost hope in the world. I feel like a numb zombie all the time. I don't want to get up in the morning, I don't eat much, I barely talk to my friends. I don't know what's wrong. Maybe it's the fact that my dad don't care anymore. He'd rather be off with his new "girlfriend." Or maybe it's the fact that I can't even feel happy anymore. Maybe it's the fact that I'm the sickest person ever, I'm always in the hospital or going to the doctor or doing 10,000 X-rays and Cat-scans. . . . I never wanna have fun. I feel and look like crap, or maybe it's my ever-so-perfect grandparents always expecting way too much of me. I hate knowing that I've failed them, but I just don't have the energy I used to. I no longer believe that everything is going to be all right, because it's not. Nothing is ever going to be the same ever again. . . . Everyone is just pretending to be happy, putting fake smiles on their faces so other people don't see their pain . . . but I do. I can see right through their little fronts. I never used to be like this, so mean and cold. I feel heartless. I don't know what happened to me.*

Still, there are signs of hope and proof that a good teacher can make a difference. The girl who wrote the harrowing poem gave this letter to Howe:

> *I would like to thank you for being there for me this whole semester. I have learned that there is always someone that is*

going to be there and that must care. And I would also want to thank you for all the gifts you have given me. I have been cherishing them and I will forever. For this upcoming semester, umm . . . I am going to start treatment for my alcoholism and I know it is going to be hard, but I have to be there for my siblings when they get older. . . . I never thought that I would actually be talking to my mom again. It's because of those things that you told me when I first came to school. Just recently I thought of cutting, but I thought about what you said, and I talked to my boyfriend, and I don't know how to explain it, but had you not stepped in to help me with my cutting problems, I don't know where I would be. Who knows? I would of [sic] ended back at the psych ward or even back at juvi [juvenile hall], but all I know is that I'm looking forward to a new year and I know for sure that I'm going to start a new life. So, I just wanted to say thank you for being there for me. Let's just say you stepped into a spot in my heart that no one can replace.

Howe was twice asked to be the commencement speaker for graduating seniors. "It was a pretty big deal," she said. "Because I was white."

Not every teacher connected. Howe describes a high turn-over rate of well-meaning teachers recruited from around the country who started strong but just couldn't cope. In turn, students grew jaded and cynical about the churn. They learned that even the most enthusiastic new teacher would be overwhelmed and probably give up. Teaching on a reservation is not a sprint, Howe will tell you; it's a marathon. You have to be able to go the distance. Howe's ability to stick it out and her understanding of

Indian tradition engendered trust, something that has been historically in short supply, and for good reason.

The Boarding School Experiment

In the late 1800s, after the Civil War ended, it freed up the military to resolve "the Indian problem" in the Great Plains. In many cases, "the resolution" was brutal and criminal. The way the non-Indians saw it, "savages" were living among the civilized farmers, and their efforts to reclaim their land from those they viewed as invaders posed a threat.

Politicians decided that they had to find a way to assimilate the Indians into the white culture. The process would hinge on the education of the youth that would strip away the cultural attachments and traditions the youth had to their race. In 1889, Thomas Morgan, U.S. commissioner of Indian Affairs, encapsulated the attitude of the times when he wrote, "The Indians must conform to the white man's ways, peacefully if they will, forcibly if they must."

Mark Cherrington, editor of *Cultural Survival Quarterly,* explains the American boarding school concept used as a model in Canada: "It was based on the idea that the most effective way to eliminate Indian culture was to break the chain of transmission: to remove children from their cultural environment and indoctrinate them in complete isolation. To be sure that there was no chance of backsliding, children were put in schools far from their homes, in some cases thousands of miles away. Their parents were not allowed to visit, and the children were not allowed to return home. . . . The education they received did not include Latin or biology or philosophy; they were limited to trades like carpentry, blacksmithing, shoemaking, farming, cooking, knitting, and ironing—fodder for the engines of prosperity."

Imagine your cultural and family traditions being swept away—the historical pride, traditions, wisdom, and family bonds, those critical societal anchors gone. It turned out to be a brutal failed experiment in social engineering, the ramifications of which are felt today. These schools, although fewer in number now, have provoked an aggressive debate about the impact of the boarding schools on Indian children.

Perhaps the most famous (or infamous) of the Indian boarding schools, the Carlisle Indian Industrial School, was founded in 1879 in Carlisle, Pennsylvania, by Richard Pratt, a former military officer. He created a new school based on his experience with young Native American prisoners. He had taught these Indian prisoners to speak proper English, converted them to Christianity, and prepared them for employment.

Pratt published a book on the success of his program and demonstrated through photographs and individual success stories the conversion of the prisoners from what he called "savages" to "civilized." His photographs showed the differences he achieved converting these Indian prisoners from long-haired youths in leather clothing to those with cut and combed hair wearing pressed shirts and polished shoes.

The motto of the Carlisle School was, "Kill the Indian, save the man." The goal was assimilation. The school was all about discipline. The young Indian boys were required to get their hair cut short. The braided hair that was so prevalent among Indian youth was prohibited. Discipline was very strict. The Indian students were given names that would be considered "white" names. Conversion to Christianity was a central tenet of the conversion from a "savage" to a "civilized" person.

For the next nearly half century, there was a relentless effort to "civilize" the Native Americans through education at Indian boarding schools. A U.S. government report in 1928 described the living conditions in many of these schools. They included exposed electrical wiring, no indoor toilets, poor ventilation, and few sanitary supplies.

Harvard Magazine, in a 2008 feature, reported, "Indian boarding schools were blunt tools: they rank among the most heavy-handed institutions of socialization, indoctrination, and even brainwashing ever seen in North America. Scholars have described the residential boarding schools as 'labor camps,' or experiments in modified slavery, run in the grueling, regimented manner of military schools."

Pratt recruited children from the Pine Ridge and Rosebud Indian Reservations in South Dakota to the Carlisle Indian Industrial School. And from that, hundreds of other Indian schools took shape to move the young Native Americans from the reservation to be schooled at boarding schools. At the peak of the schools, there were five hundred boarding schools in eighteen states.

At the Carlisle Indian Industrial School (where Jim Thorpe was its most famous graduate), there were 1,842 recorded desertions and nearly 500 deaths according to the Native American Rights Fund Legal Review. If captured, the desertion was punishable by beatings, isolation in outbuildings used as jails, physical restraints, and more.

According to the Minnesota Historical Society, a student at St. Benedict's Mission "recalled being punished by being made to chew lye soap and blow bubbles that burned the inside of her mouth. This was a common punishment for students if they spoke their tribal language."

Even in modern times, the abuse was common. When he was

four, American Indian Movement (AIM) activist Dennis Banks was sent three hundred miles from his home to the Pipestone Indian School in Minnesota. On multiple occasions, when he ran away, he was caught and severely beaten each time. How could these experiences not shape one's worldview?

Banks was part of the Wounded Knee armed standoff with federal agents in 1973. The seventy-one-day Wounded Knee standoff incident began as a protest against corrupt tribal leadership and broken government promises. Banks and Russell Means were indicted on federal charges of conspiracy and assault, but their case was dismissed for prosecutorial misconduct, a decision upheld on appeal. That event created awareness for non-Indians and an awakening for Native Americans.

Fred Medina, a lab technician who attended two Indian boarding schools, told *Harvard Magazine,* "Wounded Knee turned around a lot of things for all Indians. We recognized ourselves as not being second-class but up there with everybody else."

After the 1928 government report exposed the harsh conditions at Indian schools, attitudes began to change, and they slowly began to close down. Those that remain have evolved.

Then, finally, with the 1934 Indian Reorganization Act, the government belatedly recognized that the obliteration of the Indian culture in schools was destructive and counterproductive to the goal of educating Native American youth. They then allowed the teaching of Indian history and culture in the Bureau of Indian Education (BIE) schools. That began a period where there was opportunity for Indian students to study and understand their culture and heritage. But a great deal of damage had been done.

Tamara's experience at the Pierre Indian Learning Center was much more positive than that of Indians in the past. It's an off-reservation boarding school for Native American children. The school is located in Pierre, South Dakota, and serves as an educational center and living area for approximately 250 students from grades one through eight annually. These students come from fifteen different tribes in North Dakota, South Dakota, and Nebraska.

"Boarding schools are not necessarily bad," she said. She remembers the dorm and kitchen staff fondly. "They treated you like you were their own grandchildren."

The Pierre Indian Learning Center describes itself as "a therapeutic model that helps all students progress through past experiences so that they may be successful in the future. The model is designed to meet the emotional, intellectual, and cultural needs of our students."

For the first time in her life, Tamara felt safe and cared for. "It was a place we knew wasn't going away." The school provided stability and many activities that occupied and enriched the lives of the students. "There was horseback riding, a zip line, paintball, baseball. . . . We took field trips, went to movies. They had something going each weekend," Tamara said. "It was a really good place to be."

She grew somber for a moment. "They would send us home for spring and summer vacations. I hated coming home." She remembered other children feeling the same way. "Kids would cry, because they didn't want to go home."

Fred Medina's niece, Kim Toribio, who was part of the *Harvard Magazine* story, said her experience in the 1980s at Santa Fe Indian School, where the staff was comprised of Native Americans, was a good one, too. "They cared about you. They'd bend over backward to get you scholarships."

Another success story about Tim O'Neal, a student at Wyoming Indian High School, was reported by Wyoming Public

Media. "I was just drinking, partying, trying to be cool," he said. "It messed with my schoolwork. My whole class schedule—all seven classes—I was failing, and there was no way I could make up the grades, so I just asked my parents if I would be able to go to a boarding school." That school was Chemawa Indian School in Salem, Oregon, which was founded in 1880 and is one of our remaining boarding high schools run by the Bureau of Indian Education. "My experience was good there," O'Neal said. "They allowed me to catch up on some schoolwork, and when I caught up, I found out I was top of the class." He graduated as valedictorian.

Tamara says that some of her classmates at the Pierre Indian Learning Center found the experience so transformative they have enrolled their own children there.

Progress, yes, but overall, Native American education gets a failing grade, and despite some successes, the BIE shoulders much of the blame.

BIE Schools Come Up Short

The Bureau of Indian Education oversees reservation schools, but the bureau has had thirty-three directors in thirty-six years. The instability in the BIE is reflected in the graduation rates among Indian students. Just 53 percent of Indian students who attend BIE schools are graduating from high school.

The disrepair and deteriorating condition of the BIE schools is another travesty. Of the 183 Indian schools, 83 of them are over thirty years old with 63 of them in poor condition. A 2014 federal study revealed leaking and collapsing roofs, buckling floors, exposed wires, gas leaks, and poor heating and cooling systems. John Kline, a U.S. Republican representative from

Minnesota, said, "You can't be well educated when you are attending school wearing your coat and mittens."

The dropout rate for Native American students is nearly twice the national average. Three out of every ten Native students drop out before finishing high school. These are the highest dropout rates of any other subgroup of students in the United States. These students are posting the worst achievement scores and lowest graduation rates of any student subgroup.

But a closer look at certain states and specific Indian reservations describes an even more ominous story. *U.S. News & World Report* stated from a report produced by Education Week that only 51 percent of Native American students in the incoming high school class of 2010 ended up earning a high school diploma.

In Alaska, the graduation rate for the Native students was only 42.5 percent in 2010. In South Dakota, less than one-third of Native American students graduated from high school, lower than the lowest rate of high school graduation of any country in the world—South Sudan at 37 percent. Process that for a moment. Meanwhile, the national average of students graduating from high school is 80 percent.

Even those numbers may be deceptive, based on Tamara's experience. She says teachers were willing to give her passing grades to let her graduate even though she hadn't done the work. Standing on principle, she refused to take what she had not earned.

The issue of how to educate Native Americans has been debated for many decades, but the elements of successful education, for Indian youth and all youth, are not a mystery.

First, school authorities and those who fund the education system need to make certain there are good schools available. Second, parents need to be involved in their children's education.

Finally, it requires a teacher that knows how to teach and a student willing to learn. If all those things are present, education works. If not, a child's education faces an uphill struggle.

The youth living on Indian reservations often are attending schools that are in disrepair because the federal government has not adequately funded them. In other cases, the student can come from a broken home or a home with substance abuse and violence. That almost always means that parents are not involved in their education. It's a major disadvantage for Native American youth.

Because the education policy has been so misguided and underfunded, the reality is Native Americans are metaphorically expected to clear the same hurdles as others while starting in a hole. When Indian schools are far short of the money needed to offer full opportunities for a good education, the students suffer the consequences. They are unprepared for a higher education and additional opportunities.

Quite simply, many children who live on reservations do not get the same education and therefore don't get the same opportunities as non-Indian children in the United States.

Nelson Mandela said, "Education is the most powerful weapon which you can use to change the world." It is. It's the single most powerful tool against cyclical poverty.

According to the National Center for Education Statistics, in 2015, the median earnings of young adults with a bachelor's degree—$50,000—were 64 percent higher than those of young adult high school graduates, who earned $30,500, which in turn was 22 percent more than those who did not complete high school.

It's pretty basic. It's about an investment in people that pays off for everyone. The more earning power an individual has, the greater the tax base with which to fund infrastructure and less reliance on social safety net programs. Education is the tool with which to build a better life.

The lack of funding affects classwork and also school athletics, which can be a source of pride for students. A story about two high school wrestlers at the Pine Ridge High School describes such a case. Two of the high school wrestlers had won their matches at the regional tournament, and because of that, they were qualified to go to the state tournament. But the school had no funds to send the two boys to the state tournament. The boys were disappointed until their coach, David Michaud, said, "You deserve to be at the state tournament, and I am going to take you there."

And he made it happen. Michaud bought them new uniforms to wear. He drove the kids across the state to the tournament. They didn't have money for a motel, so they got permission to sleep in sleeping bags on the gymnasium floor of the building where the tournament would be held.

It cost the wrestling coach about $600 of his own money to take the kids to the tournament, but what a message it sent about the value of those two wrestlers' accomplishments. If there was any embarrassment from the kids for having to sleep on the gymnasium floor, they didn't show it. They were there, they deserved to be there, and their coach was not going to let them miss the opportunity.

The most basic elements of the success of educating children, all children, are the same. A good teacher, an involved parent, and a child who wants to learn. Every child deserves the opportunity to learn in that environment, and the goal in Indian education should be to make those conditions available to all children.

6

Justice Is a Stranger Here

There was a crime that occurred here.
Human beings were abused. But nothing was done.
—TAMARA'S GRANDFATHER

It sounds almost impossible, but the horrific beating of two-year-old Tamara on the Standing Rock Indian Reservation went unpunished. No one was ever charged for the crime.

Ever.

There's not even a record of an investigation. Astonishing. A young girl is brutally beaten, and no one is responsible? Justice for all? Hardly. Too often, justice is a stranger on Indian reservations.

The thing is, no one seemed very surprised that there was no prosecution. Tamara's grandfather, a retired Bureau of Indian Affairs police officer, was furious. He demanded justice—refused to let it go. He prodded, filed complaints, but no one, and no agency, appeared to care.

Law enforcement, as is the norm with reservation crimes, offered lip service, but the fact that nothing happened to bring the guilty parties to justice isn't unusual. Most Indians who live on reservations are accustomed to seeing crime and violence go unpunished. Crimes go unreported. It's viewed as an exercise in futility.

Out here, you're on your own.

Tamara was alone, and she never had much of a chance. Imagine having to try to internalize the trauma of that beating. She was put in harm's way by different people for so many different reasons, none of them defensible.

First and foremost, Tamara was put in harm's way by her parents' serious alcohol addiction and neglect.

Tamara was also put in harm's way by social workers on the reservation who were required to work on up to 125 child welfare cases at the same time. The standard manageable caseload is no more than 25–35 cases. The result was predictable and dangerous. The foster home was obviously not properly vetted. It turned out to be a very dangerous place for a young child.

For a period of time after she suffered the beating at the foster home, Tamara lived with her maternal grandfather and grandmother. That's where she was sexually assaulted by an extended family member for the first time, a crime that was repeated time and time again.

Tamara eventually confided in an older sister about the sexual abuse. When her mother was told, Tamara says her mother attacked her for lying. That's when Tamara escaped and ran away from home. "I guess I just got tired of being beaten by everyone in my life," she said.

She ran away from the dysfunctional family that failed to protect her. It was a story all too familiar to a young child who, in many other circumstances, would have been enjoying a carefree childhood. Instead, all of Tamara's energy was put into desperately trying to survive.

After she ran away and spent several weeks on the run, she

found herself alone and desperate for shelter, so she broke into an empty apartment. Eventually, she resigned herself to the reality that she had no other place to go. She returned home to the same dangerous environment.

It gives one pause. By the time she was twelve, Tamara had been the victim of numerous clear-cut felonies—assaults and rapes—and in between, countless beatings and constant neglect.

There are many other untold stories like hers, generation upon generation of them. The cycle continues. The dominoes fall like trees in the forest, apparently making no sound at all. The sounds of Tamara waking up gasping from night terrors, unheard. The sound of a child's bones being broken, unheard.

In America.

The beating she endured at the age of two was committed on the Standing Rock Indian Reservation. The FBI office and the U.S. Attorney's Office are located eighty miles away in Bismarck, North Dakota. There's not much evidence that law enforcement, including the U.S. Attorney's Office, is anxious to assign teams of investigators or prosecutors to do the painstaking, careful investigation on a reservation many miles away.

Newspaper stories reporting on the crime against Tamara stated that the FBI claimed it did an eight-month investigation of the foster home issues on the Standing Rock Indian Reservation. Presumably, that would have included the case of the beating Tamara suffered in a foster home. The FBI said it turned over its investigative report to the U.S. Attorney's Office, but there is no historical record of an FBI investigation, and the U.S. Attorney's Office has no record of receiving a report on an investigation from the FBI.

The U.S. attorney at the time, Lynn Jordheim, was quoted in the newspaper reporting on Tamara's case that he did not prosecute. The newspaper quoted him as saying, "There was evidence that a child was abused, but that doesn't mean you can prosecute."

It is likely that this case got treated as just another episode of violence on the Indian reservation that got passed over with a shrug and was given short shrift by those whose responsibility it was to fully investigate and prosecute.

Reservation Crime Twice National Average

A 2010 report from the Government Accountability Office (GAO) revealed that violent crimes on Indian reservations occurred at a rate of 101 violent crimes per 1,000 persons annually, more than twice the national average.

On many reservations, the crime wave is epidemic. Despite treaties signed by the U.S. government guaranteeing that the government would provide law enforcement on the reservations, in too many cases, it has been nearly nonexistent. Fewer than three thousand Bureau of Indian Affairs and tribal police patrol more than fifty-six million acres of Indian lands. Each officer must cover the equivalent of almost nine thousand city blocks.

On the Pine Ridge Reservation, the poverty rate is more than 50 percent. It's unclear whether poverty and unemployment have a direct correlation to crime, but those conditions can certainly contribute to some crimes of desperation.

Even when an arrest is made on Pine Ridge, it might be a forty-five-minute drive to the jail. An arrest could consume hours of manpower.

It has been worse on the Standing Rock Indian Reservation. At one point, there were just ten officers on duty to cover a territory the size of Connecticut. Former tribal chairman Ron His

Horse Is Thunder said that with such limited manpower, it meant that only two officers on average were on duty at any given time. Their job was to patrol eight different communities and 2,500 miles of road on a reservation that covered 2.3 million acres. A gap analysis commissioned by the BIA concluded that a minimum of twenty-eight officers was needed on the reservation to meet minimum safe-staffing requirements.

Given the size of that reservation and the number of officers on the tribal police force, the former chairman said, the report of a violent crime in progress would often mean that law enforcement would show up a day later, if they showed up at all. A call about a rape or murder in progress would certainly summon the tribal police, but the sheer distance they would have to cover means they would arrive far too late.

"I never felt safe," Tamara remembered. "Response time could take an hour or more. By that time, someone could be dead."

National Public Radio (NPR) told the story of twenty-year-old Leslie Ironroad, who lived on Standing Rock. One night in 2003, Ironroad left her roommate Rhea Archambault's house to go to a party. She didn't make it home.

From NPR: "When Archambault found her friend in a Bismarck, North Dakota, hospital, she was black and blue. 'I said, "Leslie, what happened?" She said, "Rhea, is that you? Turn the lights on; I can't see." But the lights in the room were on. She said, "Rhea, I was raped," and she was just squeezing my hand,' Archambault recalled. A few days later, a BIA officer arrived in the hospital room, and Leslie scratched out a statement on a tablet laid across her stomach.

"Ironroad told the officer how she was raped and said that the men locked her in a bathroom, where she swallowed diabetes pills she found in the cabinet, hoping that if she was unconscious the men would leave her alone. The next morning, someone found her on the bathroom floor and called an ambulance. A week later, Ironroad was dead—and so was the investigation. None of the authorities who could have investigated what happened to Leslie Ironroad did—not the Bureau of Indian Affairs, nor the FBI, nor anybody else. People who know the men who likely attacked her say they were never even questioned."

Even when felony arrests are made, prosecution of them is uninspiring. According to a Justice Department report, between 2005 and 2009, there were approximately nine thousand Indian matters referred to U.S. Attorney's Offices for prosecution. The large majority—77 percent of them—were for violent crimes. Over half of the referrals were "declined" by the U.S. Attorney's Offices for prosecution.

Pretty good odds if you're a felon.

The U.S. Attorney's Office is a key to justice because tribal courts don't have the authority to sentence defendants to more than three years in prison. The impotence of tribal courts goes back to 1978, when the U.S. Supreme Court stripped Indian tribes of the right to prosecute non-Indians who commit crimes on the reservations. Only in 2010 did the Tribal Law and Order Act, passed in 2010, allow tribal courts to impose up to a three-year sentence on Native American lawbreakers.

A crime occurring on an Indian reservation can be prosecuted in a tribal court except for many crimes committed by non-Indians. Violent crimes are not usually brought to the tribal courts because a potential three-year maximum sentence for a guilty verdict is far too lenient for the more serious and violent crimes. Non-Indian criminals have enjoyed special privileges on reservations for years.

Because of that legal loophole, a wanton disregard for the law was on display during the fracking boom on the oil-rich Fort Bert-hold Indian Reservation, which borders the Missouri River in North Dakota. Oil patch workers from around the country de-scended on the community when the boom hit in 2008.

Declinations by U.S. Attorneys

Here's how it works—or in many instances, doesn't work: Fel-ony criminal cases are referred to the attention of the U.S. at-torney to be considered by that office for possible prosecution. If the U.S. attorney decides not to prosecute for any reason, the case is marked as a "declination," meaning the U.S. Attorney's Of-fice has "declined" to prosecute.

Consider a recent report that showed:

- The U.S. Attorney's Office declined to prosecute 67 per-cent of the sexual assault cases.
- They declined prosecution on 46 percent of the assault cases.
- And they declined to prosecute 47 percent of the homi-cides that were referred to them.

Absorb that for a moment. The U.S. Attorney's Office declined to prosecute 67 percent of sexual assault cases and 47 percent of the murder cases they received.

Yes, the evidence has to be there, and yes, the jurisdictional tangle between law enforcement on and off the reservation is a huge part of the problem, but outside of the reservation, would any of those statistics be acceptable? In a banana republic, per-haps.

As horrifying as they are, it's easy to categorize these numbers as just statistics. But that's the view from thirty thousand feet in what is sometimes referred to as *flyover country* by much of America. On the ground, each statistic represents at least one criminal still free to commit other crimes, and at least one victim, and the cascade of trauma that affects family members and the community as well. Violent crime affects the safety of all persons who live on the reservation, but increasingly, the victims of those crimes are the children.

When Tamara saw the picture of herself as a teary child on the front page of the newspaper three decades later, she was overcome. "As an adult, you can process this," she said. "As a child, you can't." She had the sense that they were two different people—one an adult looking back with empathy at a beautiful child in full emotional retreat, conflicted by the reality that they were the same person.

She's unsure of whether it is vague, dark memories that jolt her awake three or four times a week or something else. "I can't distinguish if it's memories or something I made up as a coping mechanism," she said. "It feels like memories, but I'm not sure." It's unsettling. There's a sense of foreboding about that dark place in her mind.

Her grandfather put it succinctly when he said, "Human beings were abused. But nothing was done." *Nothing was done . . . Nothing was done . . .* Those words echo, and as we know for the abysmal track record of prosecutions, that sad sentence applies to thousands and thousands of cases. It's not because tribal officials or parents or law enforcement officials on the reservation don't care. Most do care, but they also struggle in a law enforcement system that just doesn't seem to work. A convoluted bureaucracy is the enemy of justice.

"Let's put ourselves in the same position," said Montana

senator Jon Tester at a Senate Indian Affairs Committee hearing on prosecution issues on reservations. "Let's ask ourselves what we would do if there were crimes that weren't being prosecuted. Let's ask ourselves what we would do if our kids were living in a place that was unsafe. Let's ask ourselves what we would do as far as conducting business in a place that wasn't safe. Would we be able to do that? Let's ask just ultimately about quality of life. Could we even enjoy life?"

One must be cautious of assigning racist attitudes to individuals in the system, but there's an obvious institutional indifference toward the plight of Native American victims that has overtones of institutional racism. The reservation system of justice, or the lack of it, is separate and wildly unequal.

Because the Standing Rock Indian reservation where Tamara lived straddles the two states of North and South Dakota, there are two U.S. Attorney Offices that have jurisdiction on portions of that reservation.

A member of the Standing Rock Tribal Council told U.S. Senate Committee staffers some years ago that they hadn't seen anyone from the South Dakota U.S. Attorney's Office on the reservation for years. That is astonishing, given the staggering crime rate on the reservation, but it further underscores the lack of interest by those who are required to investigate and prosecute violent crimes.

Yes, part of the problem is structural confusion among law enforcement agencies, but another problem is simply that the federal agencies responsible for responding to crime on Indian reservations seem to treat it as a lower priority.

Law enforcement officials, both tribal and federal, often complain that crimes on the reservation are very hard to investigate.

They say they just can't find witnesses who are willing to talk to law enforcement. No doubt some of that is probably true, but still, the data about prosecution of violent crimes on the reservations tells a story of serious neglect by the federal agencies.

The dangerous combination of extreme poverty, chronic unemployment, substance abuse, sexual assault, and gangs has many young Native Americans and their elders living in dangerous circumstances nearly every day.

Crimes against Indian women are especially common.

According to data developed by the U.S. Justice Department, American Indian women are ten times more likely to be murdered than other Americans. They are far more likely to be raped or sexually assaulted than other women in America. The data describes that nearly one-third of Indian women have been victims of rape or attempted rape. And, as was the case of the rape of Tamara, many of them still go unreported. Many go unprosecuted or underprosecuted because of the limitations of tribal courts.

The Violence Against Women Act passed by Congress in 2016 may finally ensure some justice for those women on the reservation who are sexually attacked by non-Indians. However, while that legislation gives Indian tribal courts the ability to prosecute non-Indians for domestic violence on the reservation, it did not include crimes such as rape, sexual assault, and also child abuse. As a result, justice remains an unattainable goal.

Children living on Indian reservations are especially vulnerable.

A *New York Times* report in 2012 included a story about a former tribal judge, Thomas Weissmuller, who was frustrated by the ineptness of the judicial system that failed a teenage victim:

He [Weissmuller] presided over a trial on the Swinomish Reservation in Washington State in which a 31-year-old man was accused of pouring root beer schnapps into the root beer of a girl who had recently turned 13. The girl, unaware of the alcohol, drank the soda and passed out. The man covered her face with her own clothes and raped her. Mr. Weissmuller said that in spite of a DNA match and statements from two relatives who witnessed the attack, federal prosecutors did not file charges.

Though convicted of rape in a tribal court, the man served only one year in jail—the maximum penalty that could be assessed by a tribal court at that time. The Justice Department declined to discuss the case.

"I don't know why it wasn't prosecuted federally," Mr. Weissmuller said. "I believe it was a very clear-cut case."

In 2017, one very high-profile case was successfully prosecuted on the Standing Rock Indian Reservation. The Cannon Ball district chairman was found guilty in Federal Court on three counts of sexual abuse of a child and one count of incest. Robert Fool Bear was accused of raping a girl repeatedly for at least four years, beginning when she was ten years old. Fool Bear was sentenced to thirty years in prison by U.S. District Court judge Daniel Hovland. (The conviction was appealed and the verdict was upheld.)

FBI agents and medical experts testified during the trial that the girl was so sexually and physically abused it likely contributed to the complex post-traumatic stress disorder she suffers.

The traumatized victim took the stand under a cloud raised by the defense attorney, putting the troubled girl's credibility up for question. "It takes a lot of courage to come into a federal courtroom and testify in a case like this," Hovland told her. "I hope someday you can weather this well, go on with your life, and put all this chaos behind you." Fool Bear's wife took a plea deal for failing to report the abuse.

The system worked in that case. One nagging question hovers: Was the case more vigorously prosecuted because the accused was a highly visible and powerful politician?

If a spotlight is what it takes, let this book shed light on these atrocities.

Cases Often Shifted to the Back Room

In rare moments of candor, some U.S. attorneys will admit that the investigations of crime on Indian reservations are shifted to the back rooms of the FBI and the U.S. Attorney Offices. They might not completely ignore it, but neither will they make them a priority with front-burner investigations.

The issue of neglect by U.S. Attorney's Offices came to light in recent years in both news reports and in hearings held in the Senate Indian Affairs Committee. There were a few U.S. attorneys who were breaking the mold; a few tried hard to do what they were required to do in investigating and prosecuting crimes on the reservations, and some of those who take these crimes seriously discovered they would pay a steep price for their efforts. During the George W. Bush administration, testimony given to the U.S. Senate Indian Affairs Committee described actions taken by the U.S. Justice Department to fire eight U.S. attorneys who were spending too much time and effort responding to crime on Indian reservations.

Thomas Heffelfinger, the U.S. attorney from Minnesota,

testified before the Senate that he was targeted for termination on a list compiled by the White House and Justice Department officials.

Monica Goodling, the former White House liaison to the department who also testified before the U.S. Senate under a grant of immunity, told the Congress that Heffelfinger was to be fired because "he spent an extraordinary amount of time on American Indian issues."

In fact, Heffelfinger was chairman of the Attorney General's Native American Issues Subcommittee and was the department's point man on improving effectiveness of the reservation prosecutions for violent crime. One would have expected him to be attentive to the crimes that were occurring on Indian reservations in his jurisdiction. Instead of a commendation, he received a letter of dismissal.

Paul Charlton, the former U.S. attorney in Arizona, met a similar fate. Charlton described a scene talking with his superiors in the Justice Department about a case involving a double murder on a Navajo reservation. Charlton said he was interrupted mid-sentence by the official asking him why he was involved in a reservation case in the first place.

Charlton believed then that the people running the Justice Department didn't know even the basics of federal Indian law—that the U.S. attorneys are *the* authority responsible for the prosecutions of violent crimes on the reservations. Or, if they knew it, they didn't think it was a priority that deserved attention. Soon Charlton was on the list of eight fired U.S. attorneys, five of whom had been prodding the Justice Department for more aggressive Indian country prosecutions and criminal justice reform for Indian country.

The many documented examples of the violence faced by

children on Indian reservations could be summed up by testimony given at a U.S. Senate Indian Affairs Committee hearing. Testimony from a young woman at the Spirit Lake Nation Reservation who was in charge of the tribal office responsible for youth protection described a crisis on that reservation. She ran an office that worked with youth programs, and she coordinated health services for tribal youth. Among her other duties was to see that crimes against young people on the reservation were investigated and the children were protected. Many of the children on the reservation were growing up in dysfunctional families with drug dependency, alcohol abuse, and violence.

She lifted her hand above the table in front of her to describe the large stack of files in her office that were allegations of sexual abuse of children, which had never even been investigated. At that point in her testimony, she began to cry. She was embarrassed at crying and apologized for it, but she could not stop sobbing. These children are still in danger, and no one seems to care, she said.

She also said the children who need mental health care can only get it with a forty-five-minute trip to a nearby city where the mental health treatment would be available, and to take a child to that treatment, she would need to borrow a car from someone at the tribal office, and that isn't always easy to do. The result is the children on the reservation are not getting the health care they need.

That absence of mental health treatment available to Native American youth is deadly to some who need help. In 2009, a North Dakota girl told the Senate Committee on Indian Affairs about the suicide of her fourteen-year-old sister:

"The experience of losing Jamie, my best friend, someone I confided in, is very painful and hard to accept. I feel lost, lonesome, alone, and sometimes angry because I don't know why she did this while I was just in the other room. We always told each other everything. She didn't tell me how she felt. I know she thought that I had enough of my own problems and didn't want to burden me with hers, but she still could have told me.

"It's been a few months now, and I still feel lost, lonesome, and alone, but what I have learned from this is: Don't keep things to yourself; talk to someone because there is always someone there for you who is willing to listen and help you."

But is there? The facts belie that hopeful statement. We don't know what caused Jamie to take her own life. Being a teenager is sometimes pressure enough. When you add the specter of danger and violence lurking around children, it can be too much.

Indian children's exposure to violence on tribal lands far exceeds the violence experienced by non-Indian children. The trauma from that violence shows up as post-traumatic stress disorder at nearly the rate experienced by soldiers returning from the wars in Iraq and Afghanistan. Consider that sentence for a moment. Indian children are in a war zone.

So what does all of this mean? And why single out the weakness of the justice system on Indian reservations when discussing Indian children living on those reservations? Simply put, it's difficult for people who live their lives without the threat of violence to understand the impact of living in circumstances where violence is all around you. If one doesn't feel safe, all the other things in your life pale by comparison.

In 2013 and 2014, the U.S. Department of Justice created an Advisory Committee on American Indian / Alaska Native Children Exposed to Violence. The report from that committee, after two years of hearing and study, was sobering. It read in part:

"American Indian and Alaska Native children are exposed to many types of violence, including simple assaults, violent threats, sexual assault and homicide. Additionally, suicide, gang violence, sex and drug trafficking prey on Native American youth."

The advisory committee heard story after story of abuse, loss, and tragedy. They heard about the legacy of historical trauma caused by loss of home, land, culture, and language in addition to the subsequent abuse of generations of Native children in American Indian boarding schools.

The report described the dearth of funding for child welfare, juvenile justice, health care, and education—and how the lack of funding negatively impacts the children. The scars are permanent. The cycle continues. The dominoes continue to fall without interruption. It's a national scandal.

A series of articles written for *The Washington Post* in recent years underscores the serious deficiencies in the system of justice for Native Americans. The author of that series, Sari Horwitz, has won three Pulitzer Prizes, but I think some of the most important work she has ever done was writing the series of in-depth articles about life on Indian reservations and specifically about the justice system, or lack of it, in Indian country. Her reporting, which was later released as a book, described a legal system in Indian country that fails to protect the children, the elderly, and the most vulnerable in the Indian population, and brought at long last some nationwide attention to these important issues.

The promises of law enforcement on Indian reservations have been hollow promises for many decades. The government has plenty to answer for in the suffering of victims who have suffered the consequences. Mark Twain once said, "There are a thousand excuses for failure, but never a good reason."

This failure falls on many shoulders—the FBI and the U.S.

attorneys and their failure to investigate and prosecute violent crimes. But it also points to the failure of presidents and Congress, who have consistently refused to provide the funding that would have kept the promise of adequate law enforcement.

Tamara's family, the justice system, and the social services system all failed Tamara again and again. None of them paid a price for it. But she did. And she still is!

The advisory committee report substantiated what many have known all along—that violence has a devastating impact on child development and can have a lasting impact on basic cognitive, emotional, and neurological functions.

How in the world could Tamara, a victim of regular abuse, the victim of felonies, possibly function in any normal fashion? Positive role models were few and far between.

She's a survivor. But in the absence of any normalcy, how can she thrive as a member of society? Beneath scar upon scar, her intellect and basic decency are obvious, but her future is still uncertain. There are thousands of Tamaras out there who need our help.

7

The Next Generation of Leaders

True leadership is only possible
when character is more important than authority.
—JOSEPH MARSHALL III, LAKOTA
SIOUX, *THE POWER OF FOUR: LEADERSHIP*
LESSONS OF CRAZY HORSE

This is a book that describes the difficult circumstances on many Indian reservations that should challenge all of us to take action.

The relentless poverty existing on too many reservations is not some mysterious disease for which there is no cure. Surely our country can summon the will to address the inequality of opportunity that exists for Native Americans.

Every day, there are parents and tribal officials making valiant efforts toward real change that will improve lives for Native Americans, but they need help. And the good news is that help is on the way in the form of exciting new leadership, coming from some very special young Native Americans who are active, involved, and are doing things that inspire all of us.

There is an old saying: "Bad news travels halfway around the world before good news gets its shoes on." It is almost always the case, and it is certainly true with respect to Native Americans. This book has delivered no small amount of bad news, but that news is required by an honest and full description of the difficulties and challenges faced by Native Americans. Identifying a problem is often the first and the easiest step. Finding solutions is more challenging. And the circumstances on the many Indian reservations are not all the same.

There are examples of reservations that have made progress and proved the resilience to prevail. In many cases, it has to do with the successful development of energy or the proximity to major population centers where they could develop an aggressive business plan. Still, many other reservations have not been as fortunate.

But it would be a mistake not to recognize and highlight some of the good news offered by the actions of young leaders who are doing innovative and important things every day to improve the lives of Native Americans. Their actions form the foundation for solutions that can be the beginning of transformational change.

I wish every American could meet the young people I've cited in this chapter. They are the emerging leaders for a new generation, and I know they are going to have a major impact on public policy for decades to come. The work they are doing is both exciting and inspiring!

Mariah Gladstone: A Passion for Good Health

Mariah Gladstone is mentioned briefly in the earlier chapter about health care, but what she is doing deserves much more notice.

You may have seen Mariah Gladstone on a TEDx Talk or maybe on YouTube talking about her project called Indigikitchen. If so, you would have seen the poise, passion, and commitment she has for improving the health of Native Americans. It is the type of leadership that offers hope for a better future for all Native Americans.

Mariah is a descendant of the Blackfeet Nation in Montana. She is a recent graduate of Columbia University with a degree in environmental engineering. Now she is back in Montana working with AmeriCorps on a climate action plan.

Mariah is an engineer by training, but her driving passion is teaching other Native Americans how to improve their health by accessing and preparing the foods that American Indians have been consuming for ten thousand years. She is doing that through a series of programs on YouTube and social media.

She knows firsthand the difficulty American Indian families have in finding access to affordable and quality foods. On her reservation, Mariah lived thirty miles from the nearest grocery store. In addition to the distance from a grocery store being a barrier, the expense of purchasing fresh and healthy foods in the store is difficult for many people. That means poverty-stricken families often having poorer health because of access and cost issues.

You are what you eat. Science tells us that.

The destruction of traditional foodways and the multigenerational dependence on government food programs have left many without the skills to access or prepare indigenous foods, and Mariah is on a mission to change that.

Her memories are of summers on the reservation when her cousins would hunt wild game and her family would eat barbecued moose ribs, elk, deer, pheasants, and other wild game. She remembers building a hoop house with hanging baskets and a raised bed with a tarp to create a greenhouse effect for growing fruits and vegetables.

"The rate of obesity and diabetes on reservations is out of

control, and much of it has to do with the lack of good diet," she said. "What many people don't know is that you can be obese and malnourished at the same time if you are not eating the right foods.

"Cooking wild game and eating plants and fruit from the natural environment is a much healthier way to live. But even if they have access to those things, most Native Americans lack the knowledge of how to prepare them." Mariah is determined to change that.

She went to high school off the reservation in Kalispell, Montana, and she spent her summers living on the Blackfeet Indian Reservation. In high school, she was an outstanding scholar and an athlete. She completed high school in three years and then applied for early decision and was accepted at Columbia University. Although she has since graduated and is now using her engineering background to work on environmental issues, you can find her on TEDx Talk, the Indigikitchen YouTube channel, or traveling the country continuing a campaign for better nutrition achieved through natural foods consumed by Native Americans for centuries.

Mariah grew up in a family where she was expected to go to college. Both of her parents were college graduates, and there was never a question about whether she was going to continue her education. Her parents made it clear that success comes through education.

The Blackfeet Indian Reservation is located on half a million acres bordered by Canada and also Glacier National Park. It is a rural Indian reservation with high rates of unemployment and the resulting poverty. Winters bring mountains of snow and hurricane-force winds, making road closures a regular occurrence. Consequently, accessibility to heating oil and groceries is limited.

Although there is already substantial cattle ranching on the reservation, the community is working to diversify the economy. The tribal government is considering building a locally owned meat-processing plant to reduce the cost of transportation and to market a Blackfeet Beef brand that would create new jobs on the reservation and also develop a marketing opportunity for locally raised meat.

Mariah is a proud Pikuni woman and is dedicated to continuing revitalizing traditional indigenous foods to combat obesity, malnutrition, and other related health problems. Her innovative programs on Indigikitchen demonstrate the kind of leadership that offers hope for a better future.

Noah Hotchkiss: Tribal Adaptive Organization

His life changed in an instant. He was nine years old, sitting in the back seat of the car, when the head-on car crash occurred. His stepmother was killed, and the other three passengers were badly injured.

Noah Hotchkiss's injuries were the most severe of the survivors. The accident left him paralyzed from the waist down. He was told he would likely be confined to a wheelchair for the rest of his life, devastating news to an athletic young boy who loved to play soccer, football, and basketball. But Noah Hotchkiss wasn't the type to give up.

In the years following, he did experience all the expected emotions of depression and questions about his worth and future because of his confinement to a wheelchair. He wondered, *What's my place?* and *What can I do?* Somehow, showing unusual spirit and determination, he conquered those feelings and, at a young age, has demonstrated a remarkable record of accomplishment.

Noah Hotchkiss discovered something called *adaptive sports,* and he pursued it with a fierce determination. He became a mono skier, holding national titles in downhill ski racing. He was the first paraplegic to complete the grueling seven-day mountain bike ride from Telluride, Colorado, to Moab, Utah. He has also become an accomplished wheelchair basketball player—good enough to be recruited to play NCAA Division I wheelchair basketball at the University of Illinois.

But those accomplishments only touch on the extraordinary drive and determination of Noah Hotchkiss. In high school, Noah secured funding from Billy Mills's Dreamstarter Academy to launch the Tribal Adaptive Organization that uses adaptive sports like wheelchair basketball camps and mono skiing to address the needs and promote the strengths of Native Americans with disabilities. He's using sports as a tool to build independence and responsibility and has worked with tribes to create a more disability-friendly future in Indian country.

"Ironically, it was my injury that taught me something that is most important to me," Noah said. "Our challenges and obstacles are our greatest teachers and can often offer other opportunities in our lives.

"Disabled-friendly sports for youth are expensive," Noah said. "It requires commitment from families, trainers, coaches, and others to succeed. But many families lack the financial resources and the time to devote to the endless doctors' appointments and the training and coaching that is required for disabled athletes. My father drove sixteen hours round trip so I could practice and play wheelchair basketball. I want to help other Native American youth with disabilities to discover what I have discovered. Adaptive sports can be rewarding and can open new opportunities for people with disabilities."

Noah credits his family, especially his father, uncles, and grandfather, for teaching him the traditional, Native American culture that became the foundation and inspiration for what he has accomplished.

His family has suffered some of the typical challenges faced by many Native American families, including diabetes, alcoholism, substance abuse, and suicide, so he is acutely aware of the challenges many Native Americans face, and he is committed to being one of the Indian leaders who can address these challenges. Noah said that he has drawn special inspiration from his younger sister, Amanda, who was in the same car accident and injured her femur growth plate at age eight.

"It caused major problems with her leg and knee, and she was never able to play sports because of it. She has had a difficult life and significant struggles and was hospitalized once for six months because of her mental health issues," he said. "But she is doing so much better now, and she joined my old wheelchair basketball team. I will never forget how excited she was when she called me to say, 'I'm on a team!' My little sister was the only one who never treated me any differently before and after my accident, and she is my hero for that. Now she is my inspiration to continue with adaptive sports so our community will learn how it can change lives."

Noah's positive outlook is infectious.

In addition to adaptive sports, Noah has become a strong advocate of better health care as a result of his injury. Those with serious injuries and health problems have to be able to rely on better health care. That is especially true for Native Americans who often find out-of-date equipment, poor physical therapy, long waiting times, and inferior health as barriers to recovery.

Noah Hotchkiss is just getting started. When he completes

his college education, he intends to concentrate on building his Tribal Adaptive Organization to provide opportunities to other Native American youth with disabilities.

Josie Raphaelito: A Champion for Change

When Josie Raphaelito walked across the stage at George Washington University in Washington, D.C., to receive her master's degree in public health, she was continuing a long journey that started in a small town on an Indian reservation in New Mexico.

A community member of the Ramah Navajo Indian Reservation, Josie worked hard and excelled at school in everything she tried. She graduated as the valedictorian of a high school class of twenty-six students with a 4.0 grade point average and was the captain of her high school volleyball team.

She was accepted to Brown University in Rhode Island but decided to enroll at the University of New England in Maine. After achieving her bachelor's degree, she moved to Washington, D.C., and received her master's degree at George Washington University.

That is the route that brought her to become a senior program manager at the Center for Native American Youth where she worked on teen suicide prevention, education opportunity, and more. Josie's work at the Center for Native American Youth demonstrated her leadership in reaching out and helping other youth to achieve their dreams.

Josie began a program called Champions for Change that searched for young Native Americans who were doing exceptional and positive things to help other people, a program that celebrated the good news about Native American youth and identified some exceptional young people who will become future leaders.

So what are the things present in the lives of some Native American youth that move some to the heights of academic and professional achievement, while others have trouble finding their footing on the first step of the ladder?

"I came from a town of twenty-one hundred people on our reservation where we had a strong education system because our tribe was one of the first to apply for self-determination funding to manage their school," Josie said. "There was poverty in Pine Hill, but the strong school system was an important anchor for many young people," she said.

"My mother was an elementary school teacher, so I was acutely aware of my responsibility to do well and make the most of my education. She is a strong woman who raised three kids and worked hard to make ends meet. My parents divorced when I was in fifth grade, but I always continued to have a close relationship with both my mom and dad. And in many ways, they taught me so much about important things.

"My older sister, my older brother, and I all graduated from high school at the top of our class. My brother and sister were smart, athletic, and excelled in school, and that set a high bar for me. The important thing was that we all ran with a pretty engaged crowd. And that is the way to have a positive experience."

Josie said that the poverty and other problems in Pine Hill, including school dropouts and substance abuse, continue to serve as barriers to success. She described the roles her parents played in her life by pointing to the discipline her mother required in education and the expectation that they would do well. Her dad, on the other hand, taught them other types of self-discipline, and he insisted they do well at whatever they do. She said they would chop wood in the country with their father, and then he would have them get out of the pickup truck on the way home and run a mile down the road where he was waiting with the truck. He wanted them to be fit in both mind and body and to take care of each other.

"My dad battled a drinking problem, but he was always a great father, and I will always thank him for inspiring us to be the best," Josie said.

As an American Indian, she encountered racism in many forms. "Navajos are all drunks" was a comment that cut deep one day while riding in a car with friends. She had heard this generalization many times before and since. In college, she was asked if Indians still lived in tepees. Racism is alive in too many forms, she says, and it is too often present as a negative voice in the lives of Native Americans today.

Josie came from a large extended family with many cousins. Some of them lived with ten kids in a two-bedroom home without running water. Hauling water is just a way of life for some, but still, their families never felt like they were less fortunate because they shared a lot of love and support.

What is it that inspired Josie to walk across the university stage and collect a master's degree at one of our nation's best universities? What has allowed Josie to achieve while others either hold back or are held back by other circumstances?

An involved, loving family and the determination to learn and achieve. The instillation of discipline, values, and expectations at a young age and a supportive community that established a strong sense of identity as a Navajo citizen. These gifts, combined with the gifts within her, placed her on a path to success.

The journey for Josie has been rewarding, both for her personally and for so many other Native American youth that she has worked with and mentored over the years. Her work with Native American youth will continue. Josie is one of those young Native Americans who is giving back and whose talents mark her as a Native American leader.

Faith Holyan: #codepurple

At age seventeen, Faith Holyan experienced what many other Native American youth have felt after learning that a friend had taken his own life.

Faith was a bright, successful young woman who had been, at an early age, a competitor and a national champion in the Indian National Finals Rodeo circuit competing in barrel racing and breakaway roping. She made friends easily and had many acquaintances among her fellow competitors in the rodeo circuit.

One evening, while Faith was leaving for rodeo practice, she received a text from a close friend she had made in the rodeo community.

The text from her friend simply read, "Hey, Faith, how are you? What are you up to?"

Faith was in a hurry, so after she read the brief text, she responded that she was busy and would catch up with him later.

But later that evening, Faith learned the devastating news that her friend had committed suicide.

Faith was crushed by the news. There was nothing in the text message from her friend that gave even the slightest hint of what he was about to do. Why, she wondered, couldn't there have been some warning that she could detect in the text? What was her friend feeling that he couldn't communicate to a friend?

Faith decided from that experience that she needed to do

something to reach out to other youth who might be struggling with thoughts of suicide. Was there a way to raise a flag or raise a hand to let others know when they are in need of support and want someone to talk to? She knew that in her culture, it was hard for people to ask for help; too many of them face major obstacles in their lives that seem overwhelming. She wanted to create an outlet in social media to help those young people in trouble to communicate with others.

Because Faith was well known in the teenage Indian rodeo circuit and had a large following on social media, she decided to use her online platform to create the hash tag #codepurple to send a signal that someone needs help. With #codepurple, she wanted to create a social media–based suicide prevention campaign. She saw it as a way to connect peers going through difficult times with friends and loved ones.

The day Faith launched #codepurple, she received the first response to her post in twenty minutes. Her experience since that time has convinced her that she has found an effective way to encourage young Native Americans in trouble to reach out for help.

There is no question Faith Holyan's passion is rodeo; she will talk to you about her horses and the spirited competition she finds in the rodeo arena. But her other passion is helping Native American youth and reducing the number of teenage suicides among Native youth.

Faith is an inspiring, charismatic, and confident young woman who has the leadership skills that will provide guidance for Native American youth in the years ahead.

Christie Wildcat: Wind River All-Action Crew

Christie Wildcat grew up in a border town on the edge of the Wind River Indian Reservation in Wyoming. She attended public school, and, as one of only a few Native Americans in school, she could see and feel the tensions that existed between those who lived on the reservation and those non-Indians who lived in the nearby communities.

Christie Wildcat was a proud member of the Northern Arapaho tribe and beginning early in her life was drawn to the history and traditions of Native Americans. She felt that much of the tension that existed between Indians and non-Indians came from a lack of information about each other's culture. Each had negative stereotypes of the other, something Christie felt could be overcome if people worked together and better understood each other.

In high school, Christie and her cousin created an organization called the Wind River All-Action Crew. She recruited friends, both Indian and non-Indian, to join. Christie believed that a lifelong commitment to community service could begin creating the bond to bring people closer together.

"I had eighteen first cousins, so I was able to organize the Indian youth side quickly. And then we added the non-Indian students. We began our work with small projects. They included walking the dogs at the dog shelter. We made cards and brought books to the senior citizens at the Senior Citizens Manor. We did hospice visits and baked cookies for the VA. We donated our time to clean kennels at the animal shelter. We also considered ourselves as 'earth ambassadors through unity,' so we began distributing flowers and seed packets to restore some vegetation and color to our reservation and our community.

"At our school, we worked with the school board to find ways to raise awareness of our Native culture. We persuaded them to change the school's holiday name from Columbus Day to Native American Day."

The Wind River All-Action Crew was a positive force in bringing people together and providing a better understanding between Indians and non-Indians living on and near the reservation.

Christie is also an accomplished artist, and she used her artistic skill in high school by creating posters depicting the Trail of Tears, the Sand Creek Massacre, the Battle at Wounded Knee, the boarding school era, and other scenes that call attention to the treatment of Native Americans over many decades. She wanted the non-Indian students to understand that important history.

While her sister continues the Wind River All-Action Crew, Christie is now an athlete and scholar at the University of Wyoming, studying anthropology and indigenous law. She has spent time in both New Zealand and Hawaii studying indigenous populations that live there.

I am certain Christie Wildcat is destined to become a future Native American leader. Her passion to tell the story of Native Americans will bring people together.

Bobbi Jean Three Legs: Just Do It

Bobbi Jean Three Legs is a young mother who lives in a small house in Wakpala, South Dakota, a town with five streets and only 250 people, on the south end of the Standing Rock Indian Reservation, where she attends a tribal college, studying law enforcement.

She became aware of the controversy that was erupting between the reservation and the pipeline company that was building the Dakota Access Pipeline under the Missouri River to transport oil across the state (which I'll explore more thoroughly in the next chapter). Although she hadn't studied all the complex issues with the pipeline, she decided that she was going to learn about them. She wondered what she could do to be helpful.

"My little daughter always asks for a drink of water when she wakes up from her sleep," Bobbi Jean said. "Then one day, I thought about how much we take for granted that the water will always be there for my daughter, and I decided that I didn't want her facing a future that threatened our water supply."

Bobbi Jean decided then and there that she was going to do something to support those who were protesting the siting of the oil pipeline under the river that supplied water to her hometown.

"I decided to do a run to call attention to the pipeline issue. I really hadn't been a runner, but I knew it was something I could do. And I thought I might be able to attract other young people to join me. I decided to do an eleven-mile run from Wakpala to Mobridge in South Dakota just to get people involved in the issue and support our tribe," she said, "and that's the way it started for me."

And so she gathered up the young kids from the basketball team she was coaching and passed leaflets to the 130 homes in Wakpala. She recruited thirty runners ranging in age from six to sixty, but most were young people.

In a light rain on a Saturday morning, they began the eleven-mile run. They ran on the road that follows the Missouri River, which meanders down from Fort Yates to Wakpala. On the river, there were two young people who followed the run in their canoes.

At the start of the run, her grandfather prayed for the group, telling them that the spirit of the water would follow them on their run. The young people that followed Bobbi Jean that day were excited to be doing something that they hoped would help the tribe in the protest.

A week after the inspirational run to Mobridge, Bobbi Jean Three Legs wasn't through. She wanted to do more. So she decided to visit the Sacred Stone Camp that had been set up outside of Fort Yates on the Indian reservation to protest the pipeline.

The people at the camp heard she had led a run in South Dakota, and the organizers at the camp asked her to lead a youth run to Omaha, Nebraska, to bring a petition to the U.S. Army Corps of Engineers, who has authority over construction of such pipelines.

"I knew that if I volunteered to do that, it was a much greater commitment than the short eleven-mile run between Wakpala and Mobridge, South Dakota, but I was excited and anxious to organize that run with other youth. Before we knew it, there were four of us planning to leave the Sacred Stone Camp to begin the five-hundred-mile run to Omaha, Nebraska," she said.

"The night before we left, we danced and celebrated the run, and we raised money from small donations offered by people at Standing Rock. We raised $358, and it was all the money we had. It was gone after the first day," Bobbi Jean said. "But somehow, every place we went on our run, they contributed. Money, food, places to stay . . . The support we received everywhere was unbelievable."

Bobbi Jean and four other runners left on April 24 to deliver a petition of opposition to the pipeline to the U.S. Army Corps of Engineers.

Bobbi Jean, Joseph White Eyes, and the other youth adopted

the crow-hop relay style of running in which they would run a short distance (up to one mile) on foot, then exchange places with another runner who runs the same distance.

Running was a cultural tradition over the long history of Native tribes. Before Europeans brought horses to the new country, Indian long-distance runners routinely delivered messages to and from the Sioux tribes across the Great Plains. Before the age of automobiles, Indian runners who were resting were carried on horseback, but now they rode in a van. Twelve runners (they had gathered new runners along the way) reached Omaha in just eight days.

On the morning of May 3, they presented their petition opposing the pipeline route to the Corps of Engineers official who met them on the steps of the Corps Omaha office. They learned later that the official who met them on the steps was not the director; he had delegated that job to an underling.

During the run to Omaha, they learned that the corps had already approved the pipeline route, but the runners continued anyway, insistent on handing the corps that petition on the steps of the corps office, symbolizing an unwillingness to give up.

When they returned, Bobbi Jean and her fellow runners were celebrated for the run to deliver the petitions to Omaha. The run had become a powerful symbol of the pipeline protest.

It was a strong and memorable message to the U.S. government from sovereign Indian nations, but Bobbi Jean Three Legs and the other youth weren't done.

In a few weeks, they were restless, and they decided they were going to run the two thousand miles to Washington, D.C., and deliver a petition with 140,000 signatures opposing the pipeline route to the U.S Army Corps of Engineers headquarters.

And so preparations began for the long journey to the nation's capital. On July 15, thirty runners left the Sacred Stone Camp to begin the run to Washington, D.C.

On July 26, during the run, they learned once again that the Dakota Access Pipeline easements had been approved, but they continued their run.

Once again, they left with meager resources to pay for the trip, but they found generosity at every step of the trip. The American people reached out to help the runners with shelter and food and funding. The run to Washington, D.C., took twenty-eight days to complete. When they reached Washington, D.C., they marched down Constitution Avenue to present their protest petition to the corps.

The protest and the run awakened the country to the controversy and generated international support; even the pope weighed in on the side of fair treatment for Native Americans. That run by the young Native Americans stirred the conscience of the American people on the shameful treatment of Native Americans and became a powerful example of youth involvement in a time of need.

When President Trump took office in January of 2017, he immediately issued final approval for the pipeline routing under the Missouri River. Although the protest at the Standing Rock Indian Reservation did not end up stopping the pipeline under the river, the standoff was not in vain; it became an important opportunity linking the treatment of Native Americans over the past two centuries to building a coalition for progress in the decades ahead.

The run by Bobbi Jean Three Legs and the other youth was an important symbol of that determination.

8

Leadership

It is our responsibility as tribal leaders to be the role models for Native American youth. We are the ones who have to find new ideas and new solutions to solve the chronic problems of poverty, unemployment, school dropouts, and teen suicide. To accomplish that, we need to give youth a voice and a place at the table to help us frame the new solutions to old problems. I am convinced we can do this.

—JOE GARCIA, FORMER PRESIDENT OF
THE CONGRESS OF AMERICAN INDIANS

It is fair to ask the questions: Where is the leadership? Who is responsible for the conditions that too many of the First Americans face? How can these have been allowed to worsen for decades?

This book describes the nearly insurmountable obstacles that have been put in the way of those who aspire to lead.

And it also describes areas where there has been a failure of leadership for many different reasons. There are some circumstances where Indian leaders have to own the failures. The Indian tribal leadership in some areas has fallen far short of what is needed. As mentioned previously in the book, the merry-go-round of leaders in and out of office on some reservations means that there is a lack of consistent long-term planning to tackle the difficult challenges.

But it is important to balance that reality by highlighting the many other examples of strong leadership by some very special Native American leaders who have been working valiantly to address these problems for many years.

Although this book paints a difficult and challenging picture of the lives of many Native Americans, it is also the case that there are some extraordinary Native American men, women, and youth, on and off the reservations, who are demonstrating inspiring leadership every day, in every way, to make lives better for all Native Americans.

There are also many Indian communities where there has been major progress and success in creating new opportunities for Indians living on reservations.

The leaders documented in this chapter come from different backgrounds and live in different parts of the country, but their paths to leadership are strikingly similar. They include men and women, some older, some younger. All share the passion to believe that the challenges and difficulties can be overcome. They are proud of their culture and heritage, and they know that the problems they face will not be solved by someone else. They are acutely aware that the burden to fix what is wrong rests with them. And the leaders described in this chapter are some Native Americans who have answered that call and have shown that strong leadership in many different ways.

Here are stories of just a few of those Indian leaders who are making a difference.

Allison Binney: The Path to a Dream

Would anyone have guessed that a nine-year-old Native American child who faced major challenges early in her life would grow up to become a leader in developing public policy affecting Native Americans all across our country? Maybe not, but that's because they would not have been able to look inside and see the steely determination to succeed in the young girl who was a member of the Sherwood Valley Band of Pomo Indians in Northern California.

Leadership is not easy to define, but it's obvious when it's before you. It exists in many different forms and arrives from unexpected directions.

Today, Allison Binney is a prominent Native American lawyer in Washington, D.C. In her early forties, she has already had a major impact on Indian policies that are bringing needed change in health care, law enforcement, education, and more.

As staff director of the U.S. Senate Indian Affairs Committee in her midthirties, she steered through Congress major new policies in Indian health care that had been stalled for fifteen years. She also led the development of the Tribal Law and Order Act that has begun the transformation of law enforcement on tribal lands.

The Tribal Law and Order Act was aimed at addressing crime on reservations with an emphasis on decreasing violence against Native American women through the hiring of more law enforcement officers for Indian County. The law enhances tribal authority to prosecute criminals.

In addition to her public service, Allison is now a lawyer at one of Washington, D.C.'s leading law firms working on policies that impact Native Americans, and she was also one of the creators of the Center for Native American Youth, a nonprofit organization focusing on education opportunity and teen suicide prevention for young Native Americans.

Hers is an inspiring story about accomplishment and

dedication. She not only has personally overcome many road-blocks that could have led her in another direction, but she has had a major influence on important policies affecting Native Americans.

The second of nine children, Allison Binney, like many other Indian children, faced poverty, alcoholism, and domestic violence. In her first nine years, her great-grandmother was the safety net for the children and a source of love and affection that kept the family together in the face of Allison's father's battle with alcoholism and her mother's struggles with mental health issues.

The domestic violence that resulted from those conditions was devastating to the children, but her great-grandmother provided a lifeline of stability and guidance in their lives. When her great-grandmother died when Allison was nine, everything changed.

"We didn't have much when my great-grandmother was alive, but we never really felt like we were poor. We were on public assistance, and somehow she managed to find ways to help us with what we needed," Allison remembered.

"But after she died, it became clear to me that we were very poor. Often we had no vehicle and used a bicycle to go to the grocery store. We walked to town and often walked to school since we were frequently not on a bus route.

"Of the first five siblings, I was the only one to finish high school, and it wasn't easy for me. I barely got through. Often when we didn't have electricity, I had to go out and find a light from the street to do my homework. And because no electricity meant hot water was not available, on some occasions I would put some clean clothes in my backpack and go to school to shower in the locker room at the gym before school started.

"It seemed like we moved to another house every year, and in many cases, I walked several miles to school each day. I wanted to get to school so I could eat the breakfast that was available to low-income kids, so I would leave at 6:00 in the morning to walk to school and be the first one there when the cafeteria opened. I was embarrassed to be eating breakfast in the line for those who had no money, and I got there early so the other kids wouldn't see me in that line."

Allison was a good athlete and played high school basketball. Those skills, and a special basketball coach, were major influences on her, inspiring her to graduate from high school. She knew she had to keep her grades up or she would be ineligible to play sports at school. When her coach knew she didn't have money to buy a new pair of basketball shoes, he found some odd jobs for her to earn money to buy the shoes.

Basketball practice often ended at 9:00 p.m. While other parents picked up their kids, Allison would have to walk several miles home after practice. Her coach was sensitive to that and would say, "Allison, no need to bother your parents; I will drop you off at home."

This thoughtful act created a lasting memory. "He knew that my parents weren't around, and in any event, there was no car and no one was coming for me," she said. "But he volunteered to give me a ride and did it without embarrassing me. The way the coach treated me was a real influence in my life and had a lot to do with my completing my high school degree."

Allison said she remembered the moment she began to develop thoughts about improving her life. "When I was a young girl walking to school in the mornings, I walked past a small bakery every day and often I saw this well-dressed man carrying a briefcase coming out of the bakery with a cup of coffee and a small bag. He always had this pleasant look on his face. I just got the feeling whenever I saw him that his life must be really good.

"When one of our teachers at school gave us a class assignment to interview someone who we thought was successful, I decided to summon the courage to ask that man who always stopped in the bakery if I could interview him for a school class project. He was so nice and said he would be happy to help.

"When I met him at his office, I discovered he was a lawyer. He described what he did as a lawyer and told me he always wanted to do something that helped other people. Out of curiosity, I asked him what he had in the small bag as he came out of the bakery every morning. He told me it was a blueberry muffin. My reaction was, 'Wow, he can afford coffee and a blueberry muffin every morning?' To a schoolgirl living in poverty, that seemed unobtainable.

"But somehow, at that meeting with the lawyer, I began to think I could do that. I could be a lawyer and help other people. Most important, I thought if someday I was successful, I could help my family. And that is when the idea began to grow that I could succeed. I would succeed! I made a decision. Somehow I was going to go to college and get a law degree. And while my journey in the intervening years was long and often difficult, I persevered. I thought if I worked hard, I could be a lawyer and help other Native American families.

"I remember the day I graduated from Arizona State University law school like it was yesterday. It was the culmination of my dream that was born in a meeting I had with the well-dressed man I saw in the mornings coming out of a bakery. It was a notion I had that I could succeed. I could make a difference.

"As I think about my journey from the poverty of my youth to the success I've had, I know the obstacles that confront so many Native American youth, but I also know from firsthand experience that, although difficult, the opportunity to build a better life is within each of us. I know that poverty and trauma affects many young Native Americans, and I understand that once we are in the cycle of intergenerational trauma, it takes a couple of generations to overcome, but I have dreams about a better day and better opportunity for all Native Americans. And it starts with each of us believing in ourselves and believing that everything is possible."

The Indomitable Elouise Cobell

Elouise Cobell was a member of the Blackfeet tribe from Montana, a tribal official, a banker, and a fierce advocate for her tribe. She became a legend, the very definition of leadership. Strong and principled, she discovered that the federal government was allowing energy companies to exploit Indian lands without paying royalties that were owed to the tribe, and she resolved to do something about it.

Think about that for a moment. Would you have the courage to challenge the oil industry and the federal government? Few would.

She was convinced that royalties that were supposed to be paid to the tribes from oil wells that were producing on Indian land were not being sent to the tribe, so she started asking tough questions about the missing money. She wanted to find out who was cheating her people.

Indian trust accounts that should have tracked the oil, gas, minerals, and other products extracted from the land had been grossly mismanaged, meaning Indians were cheated out of a large stream of income that could have been used to build their communities.

Elouise Cobell knew if she could get her hands on the records that were supposed to be maintained by the U.S. Department of the Interior, they would show widespread cheating, but those trust accounts were not made available to the tribes for inspection, so she decided to file suit against the federal government, the first big step in a crusade to expose the theft and the incompetence that had taken so much from American Indians.

Her first hint about the corruption and mismanagement came when she was named treasurer of the Blackfeet tribe. It was then that she discovered how the Department of the Interior and the trustee who was supposed to be managing the resources had been involved in what she considered a grand theft.

She discovered a trail of greed, corruption, fraud, and incompetence that had shortchanged Indians for almost two centuries. To say she was angry at what she had learned would be a vast understatement. She was on a mission to get to the bottom of it all and hold the government accountable.

For years, she could not get straight answers to her questions from the U.S. Department of the Interior that was charged with managing the trust accounts. They stonewalled her, were haughty in their responses, and considered her a nuisance. They took the position that they simply didn't have to answer her questions.

Elouise knew better, and she wasn't going to take no for an answer. She filed her lawsuit and then she went to Congress and testified before committees describing the unfairness and incompetence of the Interior Department trustee.

She described the elderly Indian woman, living in poverty in a small shack on her reservation. Through her window, the woman could see multiple oil wells pumping oil on her land each day, but she received no royalty income from that oil. She lived alone, in poverty, while the oil company pumped the oil from her land and recorded the profits for themselves. Elouise wondered how anyone could justify or explain that.

The lawsuit, filed in 1996, became known as "the Cobell Case."

While that case was pending, Elouise routinely traveled from her home in Montana to testify at multiple congressional committees. She turned up the heat on the Interior Department and the trustee's office. She brought light to the issue. She built a fire under an intractable government agency. She continued to demand a complete audit of all the trust accounts.

In one congressional appearance, she described the case of James Kennerly Jr. James was the son of James Otis Kennerly, a World War I veteran who was wounded and disabled in combat. In 1907, James was allotted trust lands on the Blackfeet reservation, and that land included deposits of oil and gas resources.

In the 1930s, the records in the Interior Department showed that the oil companies pumped thousands of barrels of oil from that land, but payments that should have gone to the Kennerly family were made to the Interior Department. Some money went to the Kennerlys over sixty years ago, but after 1946, there were no documents about the lease of his land—no statements, no deposits, and no files or records of deposits into his account.

James Otis Kennerly, the disabled World War I combat veteran, lived in poverty most of his remaining life. He couldn't afford to take care of his kids, so his son James was raised in an orphanage and then sent to an Indian boarding school.

Elouise explained that the land was now owned by Kennerly's son, James Kennerly Jr., who also lived in poverty while watching oil being produced on his land with none of the revenue coming to him.

For fifteen years, the Cobell Case languished in the federal court system. Hearing after hearing delayed a final court judgment.

Then, in 2010, after so many years of litigation, the federal government finally agreed to settle the case out of court, approving a $3.4 billion settlement.

The money was to be used to compensate individual account holders, to buy back fractionated land interests, for land restoration to reservations, and for college scholarships for Indian youth, a legacy that will live on for years to come.

It was the largest settlement ever received in a class action brought against the federal government. Federal District Court judge Royce Lamberth said something Elouise Cobell knew all along. "I've never seen more egregious misconduct by the federal government," Lamberth said.

Sadly, Elouise Cobell died in October 2011, after a lengthy battle with cancer. She succumbed to the disease before the proceeds of the settlement had been fully distributed to the people she had fought so valiantly to protect, but she died knowing she had won. She was awarded a posthumous award of the Presidential Medal of Freedom. She was a warrior.

Jefferson Keel: A Lifetime of Leadership

Many Native American men and women leaders have dedicated their lives to addressing the many challenges that come from the relentless poverty that has many in its grip on Indian reservations.

One of those leaders is Jefferson Keel from the Chickasaw Nation in Oklahoma. He is the president of the National Congress of American Indians, a strong man with the patience and skills to bring people together to find new solutions to old problems.

As a leader, he inspires confidence. His passion has been about Native American youth and building opportunities for leadership for the young Native Americans. He has been a lifetime builder who is determined to bring people on Indian reservations together to solve problems and build a better future.

Jefferson Keel grew up in a small Indian community of two hundred people, largely populated by Chickasaw and Choctaw Indians. He was one of nine kids born to parents who struggled to make ends meet nearly all their lives.

"We were poor," Jefferson said. "There is no doubt about that. But we all worked to scrape by and raise money by doing odd jobs, mowing, trash pickup . . . anywhere we could find them. We helped in the farmers' fields picking cotton, corn, peanuts. My mom worked at a small restaurant, and my father worked on agriculture crops until he lost his hearing. It was a tough life. But my dad was an elder in our church, and the church became the center of much of our social life.

"There was a lot of shame and low self-esteem from being poor. The non-Indian people had an attitude that constantly reminded us that we were poor. My mom took a lot of ridicule behind her back about the poverty. She always said, 'Don't worry about that. We are good churchgoing people, and we will make our way.'"

Jefferson Keel was a boy who grew up determined to do something better.

He excelled in high school playing football, running track, and more, and he graduated from high school when he was sixteen years old. He came from a long line of military veterans, and he was determined to enlist in the military. So, with his mother's consent, he joined the military and began basic training when he turned seventeen years old.

"I couldn't afford to go to college, and in any event, in those days, getting a high school diploma seemed like enough, so I dreamed of a military career."

He enlisted during the Vietnam War and ended up spending three years in Vietnam, earning a Bronze Star and two Purple Hearts and other awards for valor.

One of his military commanders, seeing the potential in the young soldier, advised Jefferson to go to college. And with that encouragement, he applied to ROTC, went off to college, and earned bachelor's and master's degrees while he continued his career in the armed forces.

"When I retired from the military, I saw what was happening in Indian country and knew that I had to get involved and make my voice heard. The military experience prepared me for leadership roles.

"I began working for the Chickasaw Nation as a health specialist at age forty-one. From there, I became a member of the tribal council and lieutenant governor for the tribe. I knew that on many Indian reservations, there was anger among tribal members upset with current leaders. Because of that, there was a constant merry-go-round of tribal leadership with recalls and dissatisfaction. But that constant change in leadership caused even more problems. We need stability in tribal government. The issues of drugs, substance abuse, poverty, and domestic violence can't be solved overnight, but stable leadership with good planning can begin to lead our tribes out of these problems.

"I saw firsthand that when we went to war with the military, we used all our resources to try to succeed. But when our government declares war on poverty or war on drugs or domestic violence, they don't commit the resources necessary to win those battles. That has to change.

"The grip of poverty on too many reservations creates the environment in which all the other difficult issues reside. Drugs, gangs, violence . . . these and more grow out of the helplessness and misery from extreme poverty. And the cultural trauma that has visited our people as a result of the mistreatment by the federal government over two centuries continues to have real consequences for the Indian people. But addressing that cultural trauma has to be accompanied by a call for strong and better leadership to steer toward new and better policies that will offer better lives to Native Americans."

Jefferson Keel is one of those Indian leaders who stands up and speaks out to improve the lives of Native Americans with a relentless determination to seek the changes necessary to provide opportunities for those First Americans who have been left behind. He has been providing leadership for his tribe and for Native Americans across our country for decades. But the most consistent theme of his work has been the focus on Native American youth with education and opportunity.

"They are our future," he concluded. And he's right.

W. Ron Allen: A Voice for Self-Governance

W. Ron Allen is the tribal chairman of the Jamestown S'Klallam tribe and has served in that leadership position for decades. But that is just a part of his remarkable leadership history.

Early in his life, he attended community college and then received his bachelor's degree from the University of Washington. In his late teens through his early twenties, W. Ron Allen played Indian basketball. There were a number of good tribal basketball teams that competed against each other. He was a fine player and especially enjoyed the competition. The teams were serious about their basketball, and they actually carded players to make sure they were Indians before they were eligible to play.

At one point, Ron lost his BIA Blue Card, which identified him and certified his Indian ancestry. When he attempted to get the BIA Indian identification card replaced, he learned that the Bureau of Indian Affairs had determined the tribe was not a federally recognized tribe and they no longer issued that card to tribal members. For want of an ID as an Indian, a remarkable career as an Indian leader was born.

At first, his life was not atypical. "My dad and mom married at a very young age," Ron said. "We lived in a town of about 250 people. My mom found work as a waitress, and my dad was a mechanic. They had four kids, and we had to move on occasion because there wasn't much consistent work to be found in that little town. My youth always centered around hunting and fishing. I loved the outdoors. There wasn't much excitement or drama where I grew up. When I was growing up in a small Indian village in the Northwest, I didn't really think much about Indian culture. I was a Native American and proud of it, but I just didn't focus on the history and traditions of that. But it changed quickly."

He didn't imagine that someday he would be called to leadership, but about the same time Ron was seeking a new BIA card, the chairman of his tribe had announced he was stepping down, which meant that a seat on the tribal council was open. Although Ron had not been involved in tribal politics, he was encouraged to fill that council seat, and thus began more than forty years of service as a Native American leader.

"I didn't know a lot about tribal government. Our tribe didn't have a land base, although we had land claims and treaty rights that we finally got resolved," he explained.

As a result of controversies about mismanagement of Indian funds by the BIA and some Native American tribes, Ron began focusing on the issue of self-governance by tribes that chose to manage their own affairs.

The BIA and Congress began hearings with tribal governments to talk about a new way to do tribal business. In the end, several tribes, including Ron's tribe, were able to initiate pilot projects for self-governance with tribes being given the per capita funds to begin building and planning their own approaches to health care and other needed services. Most of the first tribes to be selected for the pilot program were large tribes, but thanks to the work of W. Ron Allen, the Jamestown tribe was one of the first ten.

"Self-governance forced us to start acting and behaving like real governments," Ron said. "There were a few bumps along the way, but it has been an amazing success. It allowed us to leverage federal dollars to attract more resources and improve and expand the services we provide. We need new ideas and new business plans to build and grow the capabilities of tribal governments in the future. There are a lot of problems that need solving, and I still believe the talent exists with many tribes to address and fix these problems."

Ron's national leadership for American Indians over the past four decades has been instrumental in changing the way many tribes are doing business. In education, health care, law enforcement, and natural resources, many tribes are taking advantage of the opportunity to build their own capacity to serve their constituents through self-government.

Ron has served for nearly forty years as tribal chairman and a member of the tribal council. He has served on the executive committee of the National Congress of American Indians for over twenty-five years and served in nearly every other arena of leadership for American Indians. His life is a testament to strong and enduring leadership for Native Americans.

Joe Garcia: The Leadership Model

Joe Garcia has been a frontline leader in the Native American community for nearly three decades.

He didn't start out early in his life expecting to be a tribal leader. In fact, he was an engineer by training and working at Los Alamos National Laboratory when his tribe sought him out for a leadership position. And for the next three decades, the work he did for his tribe and other Native American people throughout the country became his calling and passion.

Joe is a member of the Ohkay Owingeh tribe (previously known as the Pueblo of San Juan). In his family, they spoke in their native language, and Joe didn't speak English until he started first grade.

"School was hard for me when I started. I had to learn English first even as I was beginning my studies," he said. "For my first six years, I attended a BIA school. Following that, I transferred to a public school. I was active in sports and played football and ran track," he said. "I remember how excited and inspired I was when I met Olympic gold medal winner Billy Mills."

Joe went to a junior college to study electronics and began working at Los Alamos National Laboratory. A friend told him about opportunities in the air force to get a commission and begin working toward a degree in engineering, so he joined the air force, and when he left the service four years later, he had earned excellent veterans benefits that allowed him to get an engineering degree from the University of New Mexico.

With a new college degree in hand, he was again recruited to rejoin Los Alamos National Laboratory. He jumped at the opportunity to return to his career there.

In 1991, while working at the laboratory, he was named lieutenant governor of his tribe. He agreed to serve but was still able to continue to work at Los Alamos.

And that began a long career spanning three decades in tribal government and national leadership. The next step for Joe was being named governor of his tribe. While serving in the leadership of his tribe, Joe Garcia was also elected president of the National Congress of American Indians.

When discussions of tribal leaders are held, Joe Garcia's name is always prominent. His philosophy is simple; he believes the federal government has a trust responsibility to the tribes. But he also believes tribal leaders have a trust responsibility, too.

"We can focus all day on how bad the services are that are provided by the federal government, but that won't do much good. We know we can do better with self-government, and that's why I have been a leader for the self-government movement among tribes for the past two decades," he said. "It is our responsibility as tribal leaders to be the role models for Native American youth. We are the ones who have to find new ideas and new solutions to solve the chronic problems of poverty, unemployment, school dropouts, and teen suicide. To accomplish that, we need to give youth a voice and a place at the table to help us frame the new solutions to old problems. I am convinced we can do this."

Wherever there is a gathering of Indian leaders in our country, you can count on Joe Garcia being there and being vocal about new ideas and better opportunities for Native Americans.

Peggy Flanagan: A Life in Public Policy

Her mother was a single mother raising a one-year-old child when they settled in to make a life for themselves in Minneapolis. To make ends meet, they lived on various assistance programs that were available from state and local government for families that were struggling. Medicaid, food stamps, and child care assistance were some of the government programs that allowed the young child and her mom to survive.

Fast-forward several decades, and that one-year-old child is Minnesota lieutenant governor Peggy Flanagan, the highest-ranking Native American woman ever elected to statewide office in the United States.

By her late thirties, Peggy had been elected to the Minneapolis School Board, elected as a state legislator, and has now been elected lieutenant governor for the state of Minnesota.

Peggy Flanagan is an enrolled member of the White Earth Band of the Ojibwe Indian tribe and the highest-ranking American Indian public official in her state. During her public service, she has celebrated her proud heritage as a Native American and has offered strong support for the important public programs that allowed her and her mother to succeed in building a new life in the city.

"As an elected official, when I hear people talk about and refer to 'those people,' I want them to understand I am one of 'those people.' I understand the importance and the value of the public programs that help people get over the rough spots in their lives. I benefited from the help offered by state and local governments to my family during a difficult time for us, so I know firsthand the value of the things we do together in our country to help each other over some rough spots in our lives."

When she attended grade school and high school, there were very few Native Americans in her classrooms. "I was always aware that, as a Native American, I was different. It wasn't until I was a sophomore in college at the University of Minnesota that I saw for the first time a teacher who looked like me. Her name was Dr. Brenda Child, and she was an acclaimed author in addition to being a remarkable person.

"During my youth, I would spend part of every summer on the White Earth Indian Reservation. The experience of going back to White Earth to spend time with my cousins and extended family constantly reminded me that there was something missing in my education about Native Americans. The real truth about American Indians was very different from the history I was taught in school."

Peggy majored in child psychology and American Indian studies at the university. Her passion for politics started on a whim when she walked into the campaign office of Senator Paul Wellstone in 2002 and started volunteering. She was hooked and, in just a few months, rose from beginner volunteer duties (like stuffing envelopes) to helping coordinate urban Indian voter outreach.

"That experience made me realize this is what I was supposed to be doing," she said. "I wanted to be working in public policy and voter engagement."

When Senator Wellstone died in a plane crash shortly before the election, Flanagan felt strongly that she had to carry on the kind of passion the senator had for policy and working for people.

She soon joined Wellstone Action, a nonprofit started by

Wellstone's surviving sons to carry on his legacy. She was a trainer who taught the basics of running for office to progressives who had never run for anything. One of her students was a high school teacher named Tim Walz, who wanted to run for Congress in a Republican-leaning district. He won and held office for twelve years before running for governor—and picking his former Wellstone trainer as his running mate.

During her time at Wellstone, Flanagan also became involved in politics as a candidate. She ran for Minneapolis School Board in 2004 and garnered the most votes in a crowded field, making her the first Native American to ever be elected to the board.

After ten years at Wellstone Action, Flanagan moved to policy work around children and families.

"My next step was to work with Marian Wright Edelman at the Children's Defense Fund focusing on improving the lives of children. Both on the reservations and on the streets of big cities, there are so many kids that, to some, are nearly invisible at best and disposable at worst. It is the responsibility of all of us to help those kids.

"As a member of the state legislature, I have made it my life's work to give hope to all Minnesotans and especially to those who are living on Indian reservations and who have been left behind. To me, everybody has a gift or a passion, and we step into the circle when we are needed and step out when we are not. This is a time for me to step into that circle on behalf of children who need our help."

That reference to "stepping into the circle" describes the mission for a young Native American child who has grown up to become an inspiring Native American leader who is making a difference as lieutenant governor of Minnesota.

9

Defenders of the Earth

When all the trees have been cut down,
when all the animals have been hunted,
when all the waters are polluted,
when all the air is unsafe to breathe,
only then will you discover you cannot eat money.

—CREE PROPHECY

To Native Americans, water is life—*Mni wiconi* in Lakota. It must be nurtured and protected. It is sacred and worth fighting for.

Understanding that simple, spiritual concept would have explained the major controversy that erupted on the Standing Rock Indian Reservation in 2016 when an oil pipeline company, Energy Transfer Partners, confronted an American Indian tribe.

The narrative spread by a sophisticated disinformation campaign touted the protest as holding the energy project hostage for financial gain, but the truth is, it was never about money. For tradition-minded Native Americans, it was always about protecting the Missouri River water from having a pipeline drilled beneath the riverbed that provided water to the tribe. They had good reason to worry.

In 2010, when the state-of-the-art BP Horizon well exploded in the Gulf of Mexico, it spilled four million barrels of oil in eighty-seven days. The Dakota Access Pipeline, a pipe wider than a big man's shoulders, could have the capacity to spill that much in a week, endangering not only the Missouri River but the Ogallala Aquifer below that provides 30 percent of all water used in the United States for irrigation.

Living in harmony with the earth is deeply imbedded in Native American culture, which takes a long view of life, aiming to protect the environment for future generations. That conflicts with a lot of short-term corporate thinking.

For Native Americans, the Standing Rock confrontation was a modern-day reminder of the genocidal forces that moved them from their lands 150 years ago. This conflict between two cultures exposed the reality that white society didn't understand traditional Native Americans and their motives. Native Americans, after hundreds of years of unfavorable interactions with white society, understood their foes all too well.

The resulting protest attracted one of the largest gatherings of American Indians in the past century. Over ten thousand people and representatives from more than 160 Indian tribes came to the campsite named the Sacred Stone Camp that was established near the Standing Rock Indian Reservation.

This was a dispute that could and should have been resolved long before there was an organized protest. Both the state government and the pipeline company had an obligation to consult with the Standing Rock tribe about the route of the oil pipeline.

When the pipeline route, which was originally considered to cross the Missouri River north of Bismarck, North Dakota, was changed and relocated in a manner that affected the Indian reservation, they had a requirement to consult with the tribal government.

The pipeline company claimed that the tribe did not object to the new route, but tribal officials dispute that. They say there is a recording of a meeting where a tribal official informed the pipeline representative that the tribe would not support new pipeline routing. In short, the treatment of the tribe in the pipeline issue resembles the same mistakes that so many have made for so long, believing they can shortchange the tribes without consequences. That was obviously not the case at Standing Rock, which became a symbol of something more than just the route of the pipeline.

Pipelines have long been built to transport oil and gas around the United States. And that will continue in the future. Pipelines are the most logical way to transport oil and natural gas, but the specific siting issues surrounding the route of various pipelines is very important. That is especially true when it is proposed near or through lands that are claimed by Native Americans. That did not happen with the pipeline that resulted in the confrontation at Standing Rock.

In a stark reminder of the fight for civil rights, photographs near the Standing Rock Indian Reservation of dogs threatening pipeline protesters on September 5, 2016, jolted Americans and people around the globe as well.

Press reports estimated three hundred activists halted construction of the controversial Dakota Access Pipeline that day. Six bulldozers and other pipeline workers retreated in the face of marchers who breached a fence at the work site. One protester narrowly escaped being crushed by the heavy machinery. The conflict took place at what Standing Rock Sioux tribe officials said is an ancient burial site. They reported significant artifacts had been destroyed by bulldozers, including ancient cairns (stacked stones used as burial markers) and stone prayer rings, an act that might be compared to running a bulldozer through a churchyard cemetery.

Standing Rock Indian Reservation tribal chairman David Archambault II said he thought the desecration was intended to provoke protesters. The dogs and their handlers were ready. The bulldozers destroyed the site one day after the Standing Rock Sioux tribe identified the site's cultural significance in court documents.

News reports described the scene. With a pipeline company helicopter and an unidentified plane circling overhead, fourteen private security officers, most clad in black, confronted the marchers with attack dogs and pepper spray. Several people reported being bitten by the dogs. One handler was also bitten by the excited animals. Some protesters fought off the dogs with sticks. While those who were pepper sprayed were attended to, the rest of the protesters, which included four young horsemen riding in bareback fashion, refused to back down.

Among the security teams hired by Energy Transfer Partners was a company called TigerSwan, whose website says it has operations in fifty countries, including security operations in Iraq, which may describe the reason for what resembled a military response to a protest.

"This is all about money and greed," Archambault said. Archambault was arrested for disorderly conduct during a protest but was later acquitted. Officially, 761 people, including journalists, were arrested during the protest. Most cases ended in acquittals, dismissal of all charges, or deferral of all charges.

The pipeline was eventually horizontally drilled some ninety feet under the river on its way from Bakken oil fields in northwest North Dakota through South Dakota and Iowa to Patoka, Illinois. From there, the oil travels to Nederland, Texas.

In Iowa, protests from farmers about the use of eminent domain for private enterprise further complicated the project.

The thirty-inch pipe has the capacity to transport five hundred thousand barrels of crude a day, about half the production of the Bakken oil fields. Railcars will continue to transport the rest. The site under the river is located just north of the Standing Rock Indian Reservation near the South Dakota border.

Lacking pipeline infrastructure, railcars carrying highly volatile Bakken crude made headlines several times when cars exploded during transit. In one tragic case, in 2013, forty-seven people were killed in explosions and fireballs in the small eastern Québec town of Lac-Mégantic when a runaway train, reaching speeds of sixty-five miles per hour, derailed near the center of the town.

The resulting inferno destroyed most of the community's downtown. Most of the dead could be identified only through DNA samples and dental records. Two thousand people had to be evacuated, and leaked oil seeped into the soil and the nearby river.

The danger and inefficiencies of oil transported by rail provided a strong argument for pipelines, but for many Native Americans, it wasn't that it was done, it was *how* it was done, seemingly with impunity, with little or no regard for the interests of Native Americans and those downstream.

The transport of oil and natural gas by pipeline has been done for decades and has been done for the benefit of moving fuel from areas of production to areas where it is used. While pipeline safety and the real concern about pipeline spills have been the subject of investigations and legislations, nothing is without risk. And the network of pipelines crossing our country is infrastructure that is needed now and will be needed in the future.

The Route of the Pipeline Was Changed

The confrontation that occurred on the Standing Rock Indian Reservation was not about stopping all pipelines for all time; it was about where the pipeline was being built and the conditions that accompanied the approval for the company building the pipeline.

The Standing Rock Indian Reservation sprawls across both Dakotas. While the pipeline was approved by the North Dakota Public Service Commission, South Dakotans and states downstream would bear the brunt of any break.

A pipeline route north of Bismarck, North Dakota, was originally considered, but for reasons no one seems to understand, the siting was changed to a place that is just a mile upstream of the Standing Rock Indian Reservation. But in fact, that "one mile" is an important mile. It represents a location that is within the boundary of the reservation that was provided in an 1858 treaty with the tribes. That treaty was subsequently broken by the government, but the new boundary has never been recognized by the tribe.

Pipeline supporters say the tribes should have contested the pipeline during North Dakota Public Service Commission hearings—something Paula Antoine and others did successfully with the South Dakota Public Utilities Commission in raising objections about the Keystone XL Pipeline.

But she points out that tribes are sovereign nations, and under the 1868 Treaty of Fort Laramie, it is the U.S. government's obligation to consult tribes regarding traditional Indian lands. Of course, the treaty also guaranteed the Lakota ownership of the Black Hills—until gold was discovered.

Months earlier, the Environmental Protection Agency had called for a reboot of the permitting process because, as they explained, "the Draft Environmental Assessment did not include any information on coordination and consultation with tribal governments other than in connection to historic and cultural resource impacts." The EPA added, "The pipeline, if completed, would cross many creeks and rivers that could quickly convey a spill into the Missouri River or other water resources and have the potential to affect the primary source of drinking water for much of North Dakota, South Dakota, and Tribal Nations. Potential spills and leaks to the Missouri River (and tributaries) would quickly affect drinking water intakes and large areas of riparian resources such as wetlands, habitat, and plant resources."

But the EPA was ignored.

Joseph Marshall III, a Lakota author who was on the march, said Manifest Destiny is alive and well in America. "It comes with a sense of impunity, the powers that be can say and do what they want to and with us [Natives] because they know no one cares, and they break the law to do that because no one, not even the feds, are going to hold them accountable," he said. "It's always been an uphill battle for us."

News reports described the scene. The day the dogs were used to threaten the protesters was a hot one. The two-mile uphill protest march was comprised of men, women of all ages, and even toddlers, whose parents carried them in the ninety-degree heat. Periodically, the lead marchers stopped to allow stragglers to catch up. Pickups loaded with bottled water provided a reminder of what this fight is about.

Pipeline opponents said all pipelines leak and they worry that a spill would devastate their way of life and those of future generations. Signs read *Water Is Life* or *Mni wiconi* in Lakota. One mother walking with her young daughter cheerfully repeated the mantra. The scent of sage was in the air.

The group was comprised of indigenous people from North America, including two Canadians who had promised a husband and a daughter, respectively, not to get arrested. There was at least one representative in the march from Mexico, women in flowing skirts, someone with a Grateful Dead T-shirt, and a number of gray-bearded men moving slowly up the hill. Non-natives from around the country made up perhaps a third of the marchers.

As the protest camps eventually grew to an estimated ten thousand people, it included various factions, including environmental activists who muted the tribes' messages and intent.

The construction site was on private property. A couple of activists had attached themselves to heavy equipment as a tactic to delay construction. Not everyone was in agreement with those tactics. Most tribal elders favored a peaceful, nonconfrontational, spiritual protest.

Paula Antoine, an organizer of the Sicangu Camp for Rosebud Indian Reservation members and friends, was a central figure in stopping the Keystone XL Pipeline in South Dakota. She reported at least 120 letters of support from tribes around the world. It was difficult to guess how many were physically represented at the camps.

Gifts and supplies poured into the campsites. One tribe sent more than seven hundred pounds of buffalo meat. Another sent in a totem pole. Firewood, batteries, water, and bathroom tissue came in.

Tepees, conventional tents, and other camping equipment were spread out over acres. The smell of cooking wafted through the camps. Port-a-potties were lined up neatly with enough bathroom tissue for an extended stay.

Each day at the camps was punctuated with prayers and ceremonies. There were sweat lodges. Calvert Swallow, from the Rosebud Indian Reservation, helped organize spiritual activities at the Sicangu Camp. "We pray for seven generations," he said. Schoolchildren and a teacher from the Lower Brule Indian Reservation were there to support the movement.

For government officials, the buffalo in the room was the echo of the 1973 American Indian Movement's Wounded Knee standoff with the FBI that became violent. Although tribal officials said they were committed to a peaceful, prayerful protest, the presence of AIM leader Clyde Bellecourt, now eighty, served as a reminder of the continuing conflict between two nations.

The divide between cultures is wider than the Missouri River.

I fully understand the concern by local law enforcement officials who were confronting a protest that was challenging and unnerving. They didn't know what would or could happen, and they were reasonably concerned for their safety and the safety of others. But the propaganda heightened the tensions for those who were required to keep order. And the appearance of military-like enforcement was unnerving to the protesters and the public.

The narrative on conservative radio and websites was decidedly pro-pipeline. Some supported calling out the National Guard. Others pointed to the oil-rich Fort Berthold Indian Reservation as evidence of hypocrisy.

Joseph Marshall said the traditionalists were driving the pipeline opposition while progressives favor a more modern, mainstream approach. "There's always that divide," he said. "There's always going to be that. The progressives think the traditionalists are stuck in the past."

For the traditionalists, one thing has not changed; they are still fighting to save their land. An old Lakota prophecy warns of a black snake that will bring with it great sorrow and destruction. There are many who believe that pipeline is the black snake.

Bill Wells gazed thoughtfully at the sunny sky and the helicopter hovering above. "I had a call from my oldest son," he said. His son told him, "I had a dream that the river was all black." It is a premonition Wells does not take lightly. He talks about the many unrecorded atrocities suffered by his predecessors. He feels their energy. "There's more than you see here," he said. "There's a spiritual battle going on."

At the construction site where the prairie was scraped bare, the air was filled with celebratory whoops and cheers when the security guards and their dogs retreated. It was not the sound of a conquered people.

The protesters lost the battle when Donald Trump, a onetime stockholder in Energy Transfer Partners, was elected. His administration brushed aside objections and legitimate concerns about the process and the EPA request for an in-depth study of possible consequences. And the pipeline was completed.

Will it leak? Of course. All things mechanical break. When? Perhaps long after both sides in the conflict are dust. Our children, grandchildren, and great-grandchildren will be on cleanup duty when the party's over.

Rationally, we know the world's current ravenous need for energy means fossil fuels and pipelines are necessary. It is also necessary, for the health of the planet and the survival of mankind, to transition as quickly and as cleanly to alternative energy—solar and wind. In the meantime, the process of energy development must be legitimate, not just a steamroller. It has to be ethical—a challenge when so much money is at stake. While the protesters lost the battle, they succeeded in raising awareness, and that will ultimately make the difference.

There are large issues at stake, including the First Amendment. The militaristic-like response by some levels of government, the use of attack dogs by the pipeline's security team, incendiary and false rumors from officials and the media. They arrested journalists. And this was before President Trump declared journalists the "enemy of the people."

The Propaganda Campaign

The propaganda campaign was sophisticated. Yes, both sides were putting out information describing their motives, but the communications from the Native American community was no match for the professional propaganda launched by the pipeline and the government.

A man named Mark Pfeifle was among those directing communications strategy for law enforcement personnel who assisted security efforts during protests against the Dakota Access Pipeline. Pfeifle operates Off the Record Strategies, a Washington, D.C.–based firm that offers private counsel with "decades of high-level experience." Pfeifle once served as deputy national security advisor for strategic communications and global outreach under President George W. Bush.

DeSmogBlog.com journalists Steve Horn and Curtis Waltman reported on Pfeifle's work with the National Sheriffs' Association. Horn and Waltman used an open records request to obtain copies of emails and other documents from the Laramie County Sheriff's Office in Wyoming. An October 4, 2016, email from Chelsea Rider, content strategist for the National Sheriffs'

Association, indicates Pfeifle worked with her and others to draft talking points that were used by law enforcement during press conferences and elsewhere to discredit the "NoDAPL" (anti–Dakota Access Pipeline) movement. The talking points document alleged that the movement was led by violent "out-of-state agitators," armed with guns and knives. It tied them to anarchists, street gangs, and drug dealers, as well as "liberal elite" financiers George Soros and Tom Steyer. Other points noted the "fear and terror" allegedly aimed at pipeline construction workers and at farmers, ranchers, and rural residents near the protest site.

In retrospect, the propaganda had a familiar sound. The so-called "invasion" of America by the Central American caravan in the fall of 2018 was also supposedly financed by Soros, Steyer, and others. Or was it just the same propaganda by the same people who used it earlier during the Standing Rock protests?

Pfeifle suggested contacting Rob Port at the *SayAnythingBlog*. Port was widely regarded as a partisan conservative who wasn't always limited by accurate reporting. (Notwithstanding that propensity, he was given a prominent role as a columnist at the state's largest newspaper.) He and several others were easy outlets for the propaganda that Pfeifle was selling.

Port and the network of carefully selected outlets continued to echo the same talking points throughout the protest period, repeatedly painting those who opposed the pipeline as violent and their occasional clashes with law enforcement as "riots." Protesters claimed infiltrators instigated violence so that the blame could be placed on anti-pipeline activists.

What began as a small protest led by Native Americans to protect their land morphed into a historical turning point—the line of demarcation when Native Americans said with a loud voice that they will not sit quietly by and watch actions by others that create risk for the tribe. Tribal chairman Archambault told *The Atlantic,* "What happened at Standing Rock is a movement, and you don't see the benefits of a movement until way later. It might not even be in my lifetime."

The protest seemed to announce the rebirth of the Indian nation, united in the traditional role that many still hold as a sacred trust. Protectors of the water. Defenders of the land. Believers in the power of prayer. A culture that reveres its ancestors and is dedicated to the next seven generations.

Chief Seattle said, "Teach your children what we have taught our children, that the earth is our mother. Whatever befalls the earth befalls the sons of the earth. If men spit upon the ground, they spit upon themselves. This we know—the earth does not belong to man—man belongs to the earth. This we know."

10

The Arc of the Moral Universe Is Bending Toward Justice

You have noticed that everything an Indian does is in a circle, and that is because the Power of the World always works in circles, and everything tries to be round . . . The sky is round, and I have heard that the earth is round like a ball, and so are all the stars. The wind, in its greatest power, whirls. Birds make their nest in circles, for theirs is the same religion as ours . . . Even the seasons form a great circle in their changing, and always come back again to where they were. The life of a man is a circle from childhood to childhood, and so it is in everything where power moves.

—BLACK ELK

Much of this book has been about a young Native American child (now a young woman) named Tamara. It is about her struggles, her challenges, and, against the odds, her survival.

Tamara, now thirty-four years old, is still suffering from the trauma of her youth and her dangerous journey to adulthood. The nightmares and anxiety still affect her ability to concentrate and to have the recovery to good health that would allow her to work.

"My nightmares have continued over many years. And my anxiety makes it difficult to be in a crowd of people; I plan any trips I take to the grocery store for two or three in the morning so I will avoid having an anxiety attack at the store," she said.

For Tamara, the harrowing journey is not over.

But finally there is hope. After the beating she suffered as a child, the abuse, the neglect, rape, and homelessness, she has found some equilibrium and stability. Thanks to an OEA program called Job Corps in Rapid City, South Dakota, she got her high school diploma. She's safe; she shares a home with her boyfriend. But the nightmares continue even now. She sometimes seems wary of the counseling that would come with a comprehensive health care analysis. "I'm not sure I want to open up those wounds," she once said.

She's three years removed from her last suicide attempt, and although profound sadness is one part of her life, she has found some stability in her life and hasn't been suicidal. She recognizes that she's come a long way and has achieved some progress, but when asked what's in her future, she pauses. "I honestly don't know."

But the good news is Tamara finally has an opportunity to get some focused attention on her medical problems, including her PTSD. An excellent community health center located near Tamara, one that is attached to a robust mental health facility, has told her it is willing to provide the medical diagnosis and treatment for her PTSD and related health issues. While that opportunity now exists, Tamara still seems cautious about making a commitment to take full advantage of it. This could be the opportunity for her to find some reprieve from her daily struggles to lead a normal life.

Although wary of it, I believe Tamara has begun to overcome her reluctance to counseling and medical treatment, and hopefully she will decide to take full advantage of this medical help.

"I am willing to do anything possible to help me overcome the nightmares and anxiety that affects the way I live," she said.

That's an encouraging sign.

As Tamara begins to seek the medical help that will now be available, her journey will change. It will be the long, patient work to restore her health.

The individual struggle Tamara has had is in some ways similar to the larger struggle of her people. There are stark parallels—a tragic and difficult history and an uncertain future.

Yet there is hope and progress ahead for Native Americans.

Their long and troubled trail has lasted centuries through harsh mistreatment at the hands of those who came to plunder and conquer.

A primary purpose of this book is to focus on Native American youth—the future—but the present must be addressed as well. It is the unsteady foundation from which we must build. So how do we shore up that foundation?

To understand the present, we have to understand the past and the cycle that was set in motion generations ago. The conditions, challenges, and opportunities that confront the youth on Indian reservations are shared by all generations living on those same reservations. Older generations, too, have been victims of and participants in a cycle of severe challenge.

While there are always redeeming stories, and a fraction of those have been explored in this book, it's impossible to ignore the myriad of issues in Indian country.

Many Indians and non-Indians have been working on them for decades. Fixing them has proven difficult because there has been no real sustained commitment or continuity of effort. There have been uneven, scattershot efforts to make things better. Good people continue to try, and some things have improved in fits and starts. Arguably, some things have gotten worse. On some reservations, the epidemic of Indian teen suicide, joblessness, alcohol and drug abuse, and failing education and health care are all harsh realities.

Signs of an Awakening

But there are growing signs of an awakening. Some of that awakening came from the Wounded Knee occupation in 1973, which was a controversial event accompanied tragically by violence—two Indian activists were killed and an FBI agent was shot and paralyzed. But it served as an early catalyst for Indian empowerment. (It happened on a site where, a century earlier, an estimated three hundred Native Americans were massacred by the U.S. military.) It was a watershed moment in which a long-subjugated people began to reassert their power. That continues. The protest against the Dakota Access Pipeline garnered worldwide attention and a new awareness of Native American concerns. To be sure, some such protests are joined by some unscrupulous people driven by alternate agendas, but at the heart of these uprisings were Native Americans with good intentions, standing up for themselves and human rights.

When you look at some of the heroes whose inspirational stories we've touched on in this book, you can feel the momentum. There's hope. There have always been keepers of tradition. Now a new generation of leaders is emerging, grounded in the past with a vision for the future.

It will take time. It will take resources. Most of all, it will take awareness, and that, too, has been the intent of this book—to tell the story, to motivate thought and action. It's been a long, hard winter for Native Americans, but there are signs of spring. Time to plant the seeds and nurture them.

Most great cultural advances are not spontaneous movements;

they are born in the hearts and minds of a few. One man, Martin Luther King Jr., helped transform the thoughts and actions of millions. But there were others around him, others that continue the fight for justice and equality today.

"The arc of the moral universe is long," he said, "but it bends toward justice." Those words meant so much to President Barack Obama, a great advocate for Native Americans, that they were quite literally woven into a rug in the Oval Office.

We've had a black president. We'll have a woman president. And someday, we will have a Native American president, grounded in the cultural principles of resilience and insight that have marked his or her people's survival and resurgence. That time is coming, and when it happens, the story will have come full circle.

The injustice against Native Americans has taken so many forms over the history of the United States, but the fact that the original Americans were identified for the first 150 years to be noncitizens ranks near the top of the list. The Fifteenth Amendment of the Constitution granted citizenship to all persons born in the United States, but it excluded American Indians. It wasn't until 1924 that American Indians were recognized as citizens and eligible to vote in elections. Shameful! They were the last Americans to receive the right to vote. Even then, some states continued to make it difficult for Native Americans to vote.

And to add an exclamation point to it, after being prevented the right to vote for the first century and a half, there are still interests at work trying to prevent them from voting.

The North Dakota state legislature in 2017 enacted legislation with new, stringent requirements for voters to show proof of residency. They included the requirement that the identifications must contain a street address. Those legislators knew that most Native Americans living on reservations do not have a street address; most only have a post office box number, which would have rendered them unable to cast their vote.

I think it was clear the legislature was trying to suppress the vote of Native Americans. Shameful!

Their action mimicked a number of other states that have enacted legislation designed to suppress the vote of other minority populations. What a disgraceful way to treat minorities!

Even with the right to vote, the current state of affairs for American Indians is still far removed from the bounty of citizenship and its benefits that most other Americans take for granted.

The opportunity to create new jobs and build new companies and industries is an important strategy to begin improving the economic health and building a better future for Native Americans, but it remains an unfulfilled goal. Over the decades, there have been routine calls to abolish Indian reservations from those who have little or no knowledge about Indian history, or frankly, no sense of justice. They often point to the poverty and crime to make the case that the reservation system has failed. But it's worth repeating that the myriad of difficulties that are encountered on Indian reservations are present in most other areas of American where they experience the same level of unemployment and persistent poverty. Those who call for abolishing reservations would propose one more injustice upon American Indians.

American Indian tribes hold unique status under our Constitution as sovereign nations that have been promised many things. It's long past time to deliver. Imagine the United States of America reneging on treaties with other nations. And yet, like deadbeats dodging bill collectors, as a nation, we keep dodging responsibility for what has transpired, what was perpetrated, and that from which we have benefited.

Although most Indian reservations were located on some fairly nonproductive land far distant from population centers, some of that land also has substantial water, energy, mining, and forestry resources that should have been and still could be beneficial to Indians living on reservations. However, those resources and the accounting for them has been the source of a major controversy for over 150 years.

The federal government's interaction with American Indians has never been well understood by non-Indians. In short, the federal government, through a Supreme Court decision in the 1800s, assumed the responsibility to manage the Indian lands for the benefit of the Indian people.

In 1934, Congress passed the Indian Reorganization Act. It mired Indian lands in perpetual trusteeship and perpetuated Justice John Marshall's 1831 assertion that the dynamics of the government's relationship with indigenous peoples was that of "a ward to his guardian." So, as trustee of Indian lands, the Department of the Interior is supposed to regulate land use and manage leases and revenue from Indian lands. At best, it is a cumbersome, ineffective tangle of bureaucratic red tape. At worst, it's larceny.

The hijacking of natural resources on Indian lands has resulted in devastating losses to the tribes. Trust accounts that should have kept track of the oil, gas, minerals, and other products that came from the land were grossly mismanaged and meant that the Indians were cheated out of a stream of income that could have been used to support life on the reservation. In some cases, the management was just sloppy and incompetent. In other cases, it was criminal behavior. Theft. Those were resources that could have been and should have been used to address the deep, gripping poverty that developed on many reservations.

Investigations have unearthed the underhanded, sometimes criminal behavior that took place under the U.S. Department of the Interior in Washington, D.C. That wanton theft, dishonesty, and incompetence for over a century finally culminated in a major federal court challenge by Elouise Cobell (described in an earlier chapter) that recovered $3.4 billion for Indians. But that was just a fraction of what has been lost.

At every turn, Native Americans have been pushed from land that had value, and when new value was discovered—gold or oil—they've been pushed out or excluded from their rightful share.

One example is the story of the Black Hills in what is now South Dakota. Technically, they're mountains. It's a majestic place with granite mountains covered by dark green pines and spruce trees that make the mountains appear black at a distance. There are a dozen native tree species in the Black Hills with magnificent canyons and ice-cold trout streams. For the Indians who lived here, it was and remains a holy place, a life-giving church of beauty and abundance.

The 1868 Fort Laramie Treaty guaranteed the "undisturbed use and occupation of land that included the Black Hills" and guaranteed that "no persons except those designated herein . . . shall ever be permitted to pass over, settle upon, or reside in the territory . . ." The tribes believed the treaty they had signed had, at long last, settled the land disputes.

In 1872, Secretary of the Interior Columbus Delano laid out his intentions:

I am inclined to think that the occupation of this region of the country is not necessary to the happiness and prosperity of the Indians, and as it is supposed to be rich in minerals and lumber it is deemed important to have it freed as early as possible from Indian occupancy. I shall, therefore, not oppose any policy which looks first to a careful examination of the subject . . . If such an examination leads to the conclusion that country is not necessary or useful to Indians, I should then deem it advisable . . . to extinguish the claim of the Indians and open the territory to the occupation of the whites.

Two years later, in 1874, General George Armstrong Custer led an exploratory expedition and military force of more than one thousand into the Black Hills. When he discovered gold in significant quantities, a gold rush was on, treaty be damned.

A decade later, in 1877, following the battle of the Little Bighorn in Montana, where General Custer and the Seventh Cavalry were wiped out, the government violated the treaty and took possession of the Black Hills from the Sioux Indian tribes. In short, the government stole the Black Hills from the Indians. Business as usual. And the government profited handsomely over the succeeding decades from the gold, timber, and other minerals that were taken from it. It is estimated over $1 billion in gold was taken from the Black Hills, polluting pristine streams in a place held in spiritual reverence by Indians with arsenic-laden mine tailings. None of the profit went to the Indian tribes. None.

Nearly one hundred years after the theft, the U.S. Supreme Court sided with the Sioux Indians and determined that the Black Hills and related lands had been taken illegally. Compensation for the government-sanctioned theft was set at a paltry $102 million. That money, sitting in a trust fund, is now estimated to have grown to over $1 billion. It remains untouched by the tribes. They don't want that money. They want their land back. A billion dollars would go a long way toward bettering Indian lives, but they stand proudly on principle against a government that has historically exhibited few principles in dealings with Native Americans.

All of this seems overwhelming. How can we make right so many wrongs that happened in the past? The answer is, we probably can't. But we can begin to try. We can begin to bend the arc of the moral universe.

Elouise Cobell's lawsuit showed that Native Americans have the power to push back and regain a measure of compensation. It showed that justice remains a possibility in America. It offered hope.

11

New Opportunities

Find your dream. It's the pursuit of the dream that heals you.
—BILLY MILLS

Just as there are new opportunities available for Tamara, there are also new opportunities to begin strengthening and repairing the larger social and economic conditions on Indian reservations.

If tribal governments finally receive some cooperation from federal and state governments, there are opportunities to create expanded economic opportunities in a number of energy and natural resource industries, information technology, and government contracting, but it will require engaged federal and state governments willing to work with Native Americans to make it happen. It is clearly in the public interest for that type of partnership to build new opportunities in Indian communities.

Reservation lands hold as much as 30 percent of the coal reserves west of the Mississippi River, half of the uranium reserves, and about one-fifth of known oil and gas reserves, estimated to be worth billions of dollars. The Southern Ute tribe in Colorado has capitalized on that and built a $4 billion fund on energy revenues, making each of its 1,400 members worth millions. They receive annual dividends. But they are the exception, not the rule!

Beyond these energy resources, other tribes also have significant opportunities to fully develop water, timber, fisheries, grazing lands, and recreational amenities that could help build new economic wealth for the tribes and Indian people.

And further, for some tribes, especially those in more urban areas, Indian gaming that was declared legal as a result of the Supreme Court decision in *California v. Cabazon Band of Indians*. That ruling has brought expanded jobs and much-needed new sources of income to many tribes.

Donald Trump, once a casino owner, and others in the gaming industry fought against the competition from Indian casinos. He and many others failed to recognize that as sovereign nations, the tribes had the right to create and operate Indian-owned casinos. (Just as an aside, many people think casino ownership is a guarantee of success. But Mr. Trump's casino experience didn't work out so well. His Taj Mahal casino in Atlantic City went bankrupt, leaving the American taxpayers stuck with the junk bonds from the hotel.)

Without question the federal government has an obligation to hold true to promises it made. But we've seen just how ineffective and unwilling the federal bureaucracy has been in keeping those promises. The biggest reason is indifference and a lack of commitment. And partly it is because these issues are not on the forefront of the American consciousness. But they should be!

One of the big issues facing many reservations is location. It has been a practical problem for a long time. Many reservations are located in remote locations far from population centers. That wasn't an accident; in most cases, it was where the federal government developed the reservation boundaries. The government says it was done in consultation with the Indians, but the negotiations were mostly one-way affairs with the government having all the leverage. The peace treaties the Indians signed with the federal government in most cases required them to surrender a large portion of their land. The properties the government allowed the Indians to keep for a reservation, were, in many cases, inhospitable lands, not very productive for raising crops or livestock.

The distant locations of those lands meant that the economic opportunities have been scarce, and the jobs, health care, and quality schools that are routinely available to most people are a long distance away. Building access to a strong society requires having the tools necessary to do the job, and many of those tools have been withheld from tribal governments. That lack of tools with which to build economic opportunity is the cause of chronic and persistent unemployment on many reservations. The unemployment results in high rates of poverty, which in turn causes the myriad of social problems that attach to poverty.

Awareness is a start, but for anything substantive to happen, there has to be developed a partnership between the federal government, Indian leaders, and private industry determined to bring opportunity to Indian reservations.

If we were to make it a priority in public policy, life could be vastly different on many reservations.

The many Indian reservations that have been bypassed in the opportunities that others have experienced begs the question: Why can't they unlock their wealth potential? It can't be because their culture is inimical to progress and economic growth. It can't be that their members lack entrepreneurial and technical skills.

Surely at the root of these communities is the culture and tradition from which a better future can be built, one that builds on tradition, adapts to the present, and builds for generations to come.

There are a number of strategies that can, if given the opportunity and resources to succeed, breathe new life and durable economic opportunity for American Indians.

Major Energy and Natural Resource Development Opportunities

Although Indian land comprises just 3 percent of the land in the United States, there is a capability for Indian land to produce more than twice that amount of energy for the country. Wind, solar, wave power, oil, coal, and natural gas are all opportunities for major new energy production.

Ironically, those living on Indian reservations now pay a higher cost for electricity than other Americans, and that, combined with substantially lower incomes, creates a significant burden. Producing more electricity near where it is needed would not only bring down the cost of power to Indian households, it would also be a major contributor of more energy for America. In addition, the development of those resources can bring desperately needed new employers and new jobs to the reservations. Done right, this can result in Indian-owned enterprises with the profits going to Native Americans.

Many of the tribes in the middle of the country are in a wind chute that makes the area a potential "Saudi Arabia of wind." In this new age of carbon restraint, the clean, renewable energy will be especially valuable. There's a necessary and inevitable transition happening in the United States to a cleaner energy future, and Native Americans can help lead the way with responsible energy development on their lands. This is one area where the location of many tribes in the northern Great Plains is a major advantage. The wind that blows over that land is a valuable resource that can be turned into long-term energy projects benefiting the tribes and our country.

No energy source is without some controversy—that's especially true with fossil fuels that result in carbon emissions—but the reality is fossil fuels, especially natural gas, are a necessary bridge to a cleaner sustainable energy grid. And new technology and innovation will continue improving the ability to remove much of the carbon, even from fossil energy.

Even with the remarkable growth of renewable energy, solar and wind power still produce less than 6 percent of all energy. We can and will see a continued burst of new wind and solar projects producing low- to zero-carbon energy. Much of it will come from Indian land producing low-cost energy and long-term profits . . . both for the benefit of tribes.

The serious implications of climate change are obvious—we urgently need to cut emissions of greenhouse gases, and in the decades ahead, the world will inevitably be moving toward what is called *deep de-carbonization* with cleaner-burning fuels.

Not everyone has gotten the urgent message about the need to reduce carbon emissions. Either that, or they are content to ignore it or parrot the bizarre claim by President Trump that climate change is a "Chinese hoax" and that it might reverse itself and "go back." Despite those who deny the threat climate change poses to our planet, the world is on course to produce more low-carbon energy, and American Indians can and will be a part of that international effort.

We are now facing a temporary detour on public policy dealing with clean energy and carbon restraint. Instead of leading on this issue, we show disdain for future generations with the abandonment of the Paris Environmental Agreement under the Trump administration. The profit-driven rollback of EPA standards is another example of that same behavior. Whatever the motive, ignorance cannot be accepted as an alibi.

Americans could learn a great deal by examining the evolved spiritual aspects of Native American culture. The seventh-generation principle is often credited to the Iroquois, but it is a way of life for many Native Americans of all tribes. It's a sacred concept that holds that all thought and action must first consider the effect it will have on future generations.

Traditional Native Americans prepare for the future, a stark contrast to a society that largely grabs what it can now and ignores the consequences for the future. Is this who we are? If so, it's not who we have to remain. What if technological advances were matched by an ethical evolution? Hasn't idealism always been part of America's foundation?

It's necessary for idealism to provide a counterweight to reality. But even as we rush toward lower carbon emissions, the necessity of gas, coal, and oil as transitional fuels is a reality.

We have a responsibility to use all energy sources wisely. One encumbrance—surprise—has been the difficulty of negotiating approval from the federal government to develop the energy resources on Indian land. The multiple agencies whose approval is required for many of the energy projects on Indian reservations make it difficult to plan and execute the progress that the tribal governments want to achieve.

There needs to be a new effort for tribal governments to take the lead and produce an energy plan in coordination with the federal government for a robust new tribal energy development initiative. The federal government should agree to streamline any necessary approval process to help Native American tribes produce, use, and sell new energy produced with environmental safeguards.

The creation of Indian-owned energy projects can help break the cycle of the exploitation that currently dominates the industry on Indian lands.

Obviously, not every Native American will agree with such a plan, but the discussions should begin. Even positive change requires compromise, and few changes are without compromises, but the Native American tradition of reverence for the earth makes Natives perfectly suited to help lead us into a cleaner, better, more equitable energy future.

Other natural resource opportunities exist on Native American lands, including mining, fishing, forestry, and more. In nearly every case, the opportunities that exist have been limited by actions of the federal government.

In these areas where there are existing opportunities for the tribes to expand their economy without outside help, the government should be a partner, not a restraint. As is the case with energy, the potential to create new companies and industries through natural resource development can be an economic boost to Native Americans. In every case, the current restraints should be identified, and the tribal government, in consultation with the federal government, should begin regulatory reform that can result in new economic growth from the development of resources on Indian land.

Information Technology Businesses

In an era of books with titles such as *The Death of Distance*, new economic opportunity must exist even in the most remote areas of our country.

With the new information technology brought by the internet, smartphones, and so many other opportunities and applications to work in the information businesses, work can be performed nearly anywhere, and the product of the work transferred everywhere.

With government incentives (including tax incentives) to guide and persuade them, the new technology and data companies could build and locate new facilities on Indian reservations and create the opportunity for jobs and economic growth for Native Americans where some of the highest unemployment in the nation exists. A government that cares could, as a matter of public policy, begin to consciously help those who have been left behind.

That could be done with concurrent investment in education facilities on reservations, which would include both vocational and higher-education institutions building on the network of tribal colleges that already exist on some reservations.

Rural economies, including those on Indian reservations, have always been at a disadvantage in attracting new economic opportunities because of their remote locations. It's hard for them to attract a manufacturing facility or similar opportunities. But with the new technology companies, including the large data centers they create, distance is no longer relevant. For them, distance is dead. So, opportunity should be born!

If, as a matter of public policy, our government really wants to jump-start economic opportunity on Indian reservations, it can, in partnerships with technology companies, create attractive tax incentives and steer the new investments and jobs from big data to those high unemployment areas. But first there has to be a will to make it happen. The First Americans are waiting!

Directed Government Contracts

The federal government is the largest single purchaser in the world for almost everything. It can create public policy that will require production for some things to be located in areas of the highest unemployment. Specifically, targeted incentives for companies with federal contracts can create new jobs in the areas of the highest unemployment just as incentives draw industry to other areas of the country.

The conservative mantra of tax breaks to fuel a vibrant economy might be part of the formula to encourage corporations and the federal government to bring new industry and new jobs to reservations.

For example, the federal government has recently made a decision to spend tens of billions of additional dollars on programs for the Department of Defense. The government could, by policy, make certain that military-related businesses and jobs be targeted to Indian reservations where unemployment is the highest. Federal incentives to produce, construct, and assemble defense materials and equipment on Indian reservations will work.

As a percentage of their population, Native American communities have sent more of their people to serve in the military than almost any other group in America. One way for our country to give back for that service would be to locate new defense industry jobs on Indian reservations.

Jobs are the key to killing poverty. A good job with decent income and benefits makes so many other things possible.

However, a complementary education system to train people to assume those jobs is necessary as well. Asking companies to produce in an area where they are unable to find the qualified, educated workers they need will result in failure.

Matching skills to existing job openings is a challenge across America. We are told that there are millions of new jobs available, but they remain unfilled because of the skills gap.

Colleges are historically leaders in innovation and training that create entire new industries and train people for them. Existing tribal colleges can and will continue to play a key role. There are three dozen of them, with some twenty thousand students, located in thirteen states that offer access to higher education to over 80 percent of Indian country. The proximity to reservations is important; it allows many students to cut housing and travel costs.

Robin Maxkii, who attended two tribal colleges, wrote this in *The Chronicle of Higher Education*:

> *The location is ideal—near family and friends—and small class sizes allow for close relationships with instructors. . . . My main reasons for attending a tribal college, though, were more personal. It was the first time I was surrounded by peers with a similar background in an educational setting. No one asked me if Indians still hunt buffalo or live in tipis, or felt the need to talk slowly to me. It was the first time I heard an instructor discuss my community without relegating it to a myth or classifying it as a historical relic.*
>
> *Native culture lives, breathes, and thrives at tribal colleges.*
>
> *Attending a tribal college has also given me membership in a unique club, made up of Native students from across the country. I became part of a supportive national network. I feel empowered by attending a tribal college, which was established not only to educate American Indians, but to continue fighting for our rights to higher education. . . .*

These colleges reinforce pride not only in our Native communities but also in ourselves. I am surrounded by ambitious Native students every day—students who might look like me or have similar dreams. My friends at tribal colleges run the gamut: 18-year-olds venturing off their reservation for the first time; elders attending school after raising two generations of children; non-Native students and international-exchange students; and urban Natives setting foot on a reservation for the first time.

Progress on Indian reservations will come, as it does everywhere, with education and jobs.

Regardless of one's philosophy about economic engineering, one irrefutable reality is if the federal government created empowerment zones on Indian reservations, coupled with real economic incentives to companies and federal agencies, it would immediately create new jobs on the reservations.

All the issues that spring from poverty would begin to abate. The cycle of despair would eventually evaporate. Would a plan like this work? Of course it would. It is just a matter of will.

This book has identified many broken promises, lies, and examples of theft and deceit from which non-Indians have benefited. But more and more often, the implied promise to all Americans of a level playing field—the opportunity to succeed—is in peril.

The gap between the haves and have-nots widens with each passing year.

One need only look at the consolidation of wealth and the stranglehold that wealth has on our government, perpetuated by narrow self-interest and not the greater good. We live as a nation by spreadsheets, fiscal quarter to fiscal quarter, with little regard for the future. Increasingly, big money, put into hyperdrive by the Supreme Court decision on Citizens United (allowing unlimited campaign donations from undisclosed sources) has perverted our democracy, and it has a major impact on dictating government policy. And those policies don't include addressing the Native American concerns.

Economic, educational, and health care issues, as in Tamara's case, mean many Indians are too busy surviving day-to-day to think much about building a future and a better life. The reality is Native Americans have not had a level playing field.

Navigating between two worlds makes it difficult for many Native Americans. Chronic unemployment is a big challenge, but even someone with a decent job might find getting a loan to be difficult. The majority of reservation land is held communally, often making it difficult to establish credit, because there is no equity.

As we've seen, when it comes to criminal and civil justice, the differences between the court systems have created a disparity that's holding Native Americans back. Tribes got the short shrift in 2001 when the Supreme Court ruled in *Atkinson Trading Co. v. Shirley* that tribes have no power to impose taxes on non-Indian owners of land inside the reservation even if the tribe provides significant services to the owner. That flies in the face of the sovereign nation status. When Americans travel to other countries, they are subject to the taxes on products and services, just as citizens of those countries are.

It's complex and convoluted. Indians have sovereign nation status, but the federal government is in the position of administrating natural resources—badly, as we have seen—and rendering judgments on jurisdictional judicial authority and issues of commerce. Perhaps we and the courts should better understand the definition of the word *sovereign*. One dictionary says that *sovereignty* describes "one possessing or held to possess supreme political power or sovereignty and one that exercises supreme authority within a limited sphere." Unfortunately for Native Americans, the Supreme Court and lower courts, in many cases, appear not to have embraced that interpretation.

The reality is, just as treaties are struck between countries, treaties have been struck with tribes, but they have been broken with impunity, and the tangle of contradictions has stymied progress.

The word *investment* has been mentioned several times in this book. To attract investment, tribes must be able to provide a reasonable opportunity for profit. When the risk is deemed too high, capitalists steer their capital to safer venues.

One solution is Native American banks to serve Indian personal and business interests, funded by the profits from natural resources, casinos, or even money recovered in lawsuits. Such a bank would be in keeping with seventh-generation tenets—Indians investing in Indians. In 2001, twenty tribes and other entities in Alaska did just that, launching the Native American Bank to serve individuals, communities, governments, and businesses. That bank's helping hand covers considerable geography. For example, it helped fund an economic development effort on the Rosebud Indian Reservation in 2015—a $2.3 million commitment. Establishing Indian-owned banks and creating opportunities for greater financial literacy is another way to help grow the economy and help individual Native Americans to participate in success.

But the commitment from Uncle Sam has to be there. With unprecedented political distractions and a national short attention span, that's a tall order. The "Make American Great Again" slogan that President Trump describes for our country sounds attractive, but it is really just a campaign slogan on a baseball cap.

So while we are considering what we are "making" here in America, we should consider making the First Americans first as recompense for the many injustices they have suffered.

Is it fair to have a plan to "Make the First Americans First"? Sure it is! Because they were here first, and yet they have been left behind. Must we keep reminding people that if you aren't Native American, you came from somewhere else?

This was their land. We took it. And the original theft of the land by the federal government was compounded by the subsequent theft of the resources that remained.

People often too casually use the word *disaster,* but when we take measure of the poverty, unemployment, poor health care, housing, and education that visits many of the Indian reservations, it clearly is a true disaster that begs for urgent help. Yes, Native Americans have a responsibility to help themselves, and on many fronts they are doing that. But it can't escape notice that the federal government has appropriated funds in the billions of dollars to respond to natural disasters in recent years. It is what our compassionate country should do to help people through a natural disaster. In just 2018, for example, the funding for natural disaster response totaled more than $100 billion.

The hurricanes, floods, earthquakes—they all are immediate, evident disasters, but a slow-motion generational disaster has impacted Native Americans, and no major resources have been made available for it. The chronic poverty has leveled many Indian reservations to no less a disaster and no less an emergency.

Young Native Americans have the greatest at stake in seeing the economic revival happen. They are the ones who leave the reservations because they cannot find jobs. Despite the pride they have in their cultural ties, they too often have no other viable choice. That migration of Native American youth robs the Indian communities of the talent and skills needed to improve lives on the reservation.

Addressing the chronic poverty through education and employment is central to real change, but it is not enough. The other critical issues of health care, housing, education, and law enforcement also need to be addressed. All of it is a matter of will and intent. Congress must earnestly begin the funding it is required to do to improve the health care, housing, and education programs on the reservations.

The difficulties and challenges on Indian reservations have existed for decades, but they do not have to be permanent. Change will and can come if our government and the Indian tribes themselves will think big, plan well, and execute to make it happen.

The predominant and generational presumption from white America has been that Indian culture is unenlightened and inferior. The evidence, especially with regard to Native Americans' traditional reverence for Mother Earth (*Uni Maka* in Lakota), tells us that is not true. The judicious use of resources, living in scientific and spiritual harmony, may be best expressed by a simple adage: "Take what you need and leave the rest." It is a philosophy foreign to our materialistic world.

Seven Generations

That sentiment was expressed by the great Lakota leader Crazy Horse, who said, "I see a time of seven generations when all the colors of mankind will gather under the sacred Tree of Life and the whole earth will become one circle again. In that day, there will be those among the Lakota who will carry knowledge and understanding of unity among all living things, and the young white ones will come to those of my people and ask for this wisdom."

Cultures evolve and change. America may be the best historic example of successfully blending cultures, although that transition, with its obvious and continuing ugly bumps, may never really be over. For example the oil-rich Fort Berthold Indian Reservation in North Dakota stands to benefit—short term, at least—from pipeline infrastructure, while downstream, with the pipeline crossing just north of the Standing Rock Indian Reservation, tribal members viewed it as a loaded gun aimed at them in an ecological game of Russian roulette.

Transition is a good word to remember. No culture is static. Transitions, if you are an optimist, are often good, but enough time has passed for the evidence to be clear that there is an ugly cycle at work on our reservations, certainly elsewhere in American culture, too, and few of those shadowy circles are as dark as the cloud over many Native Americans today.

Tradition provides the ballast of cultural identity necessary for a successful transition. One step to solving the complex puzzle is rehabilitation of an entrenched foster care system that failed Tamara, indeed, almost killed her. That's one step. The lack of justice in her case and the dearth of adequate health care on reservations have helped create great voids of inequity in a country we call the greatest on earth.

And what of Tamara? Has she moved from survival mode and started thriving? Not yet. But it is coming. Most of her scars are hidden from view. There is a tangle of emotions and harsh memories inside.

"I've just floated. I couldn't really hold down a job."

She rarely talks about it. "How does anyone give you advice on the stuff I went through, you know?" But she's alive, and that's something.

And now, at long last, there is an opportunity for Tamara to get some help, to move beyond the scars and toward a future that has been too long delayed. For this beautiful young woman, at long last, the word *hope* can be a part of her vocabulary. She is a strong woman who has survived, and now it is time for her to thrive.

She hopes that by having her story told, other young Native Americans can learn and understand that the struggle is worth it. Their lives are worth it!

What You Can Do

I believe that once you become aware of an injustice, you assume an obligation to try to fix it.

That is why, with Tamara and others in mind, I created a nonprofit organization after I retired from the U.S. Senate to help Indian youth living on reservations. The Center for Native American Youth (CNAY) focuses on teen suicide prevention, providing education opportunities, creating mentorships, and other manners of support to Native American Youth.

If you are interested in helping, please contact us at:

The Center for Native American Youth
www.cnayinfo@aspeninstitute.org
(202) 736-2905

In addition to CNAY, there are also many other wonderful organizations working to improve the lives of Native American

youth. Below is a list of just some of them if you wish to reach
out to help.

National Congress of American Indians
Washington, D.C.
(202) 466-7767
www.ncai.org

United National Indian Tribal Youth (UNITY)
Mesa, AZ
(480) 718-9793
www.unityinc.org

National Indian Health Board
Washington, D.C.
(202) 507-4070
www.nihb.org

National Indian Child Welfare Association
Portland, OR
(503) 222-4044
www.nicwa.org

National Indian Education Association
Washington, D.C.
(202) 544-7290
www.niea.org

31192021826381